D1029743

Chieftainship and legitimacy

International Library of Anthropology

Editor: Adam Kuper, University College London

Arbor Scientiae
Arbor Vitae

A catalogue of other Social Science books published by Routledge & Kegan Paul will be found at the end of this volume.

Chieftainship and legitimacy

An anthropological study of executive law in Lesotho

Ian Hamnett

Department of Sociology
University of Bristol

Routledge & Kegan Paul

London and Boston

First published in 1975
by Routledge & Kegan Paul Ltd
Broadway House, 68–74 Carter Lane,
London EC4V 5EL and
9 Park Street,
Boston, Mass. 02108, USA
Set in Monotype Times New Roman
and printed in Great Britain by
Butler & Tanner Ltd, Frome and London
© Ian Hamnett 1975

ISBN 0 7100 8177 4

To His Majesty King Moshoeshoe II of Lesotho

Contents

Illustrations

Acknowledgments

First and last, my thanks are due to His Majesty King Moshoeshoe II, whose generosity and kindness did so much to make my work possible. His friendship and support never failed me.

My second fieldwork expedition was made a special pleasure by the hospitality of Mrs Gertrude Masiloane ('Ma-Kali). She is among the chief of the many, many friends I made.

This book is dedicated, with permission, to His Majesty, and through him to the chiefs and people of Lesotho.

But even with all the help that I enjoyed from my friends in Lesotho, I do not know how this book could have appeared without the encouragement and support which Dr Vieda Skultans so unobtrusively provided. I take this opportunity of thanking her now.

Prefatory note

Superscript figures in the text refer to notes at the end of the volume, the majority of which have substantive content.

Alphabetical references in brackets on the line (Aq, Cm, etc.) refer to the List of cases cited.

Dr Basil Sansom's most valuable essay, 'Traditional Rulers and their Realms', in W. D. Hammond-Tooke (ed.), *The Bantu-speaking Peoples of Southern Africa* (London: Routledge & Kegan Paul, 1974), unfortunately appeared too late for his comments to be taken into account in the writing of this study.

I. H.

Judges ought above all to remember the conclusion of the Roman twelve tables: *salus populi suprema lex:* and to know that laws, except they be in order to that end, are but things captious, and oracles not well inspired. . . . And let no man weakly conceive, that just laws and true policy have any antipathy; for they are like the spirits and the sinews, that one moves with the other. Let judges also remember, that Solomon's throne was supported by lions on both sides; let them be lions, but yet lions under the throne; being circumspect that they do not check or oppose any points of sovereignty. Let not judges also be so ignorant of their own right, as to think there is not left to them, as a principal part of their office, a wise use and application of laws. For they may remember what the Apostle saith of a greater law than theirs: *nos scimus quia lex bona est, modo quis ea utatur legitime.*

Francis Bacon, 'Of Judicature', *Essays Civil and Moral*, lvi

Introduction: Aims and methods

This book is about law, and especially about the anthropology of law. In writing it, I have attempted two things. First, I have tried to argue that law is a specific and irreducible category of social fact, and thus to move away from the tradition, stemming from Malinowski, that would see it as only a special case, and a rather ethnocentrically defined one at that, of the wider category of 'social control'. Second, I have formulated a view of law and political action that differs in many respects from some commonly held Weberian conceptions of their relationship, and have argued for what I call 'executive law' as a concept expressing it more aptly. The aim of this book is thus theoretical; it is designed as a contribution to anthropology, and perhaps even to jurisprudence too, and not—or not directly—as a piece of ethnography, nor even as a treatise on Sotho law.

But the theoretical arguments I am advancing do not emerge from the abstract analysis of concepts so much as from the particular facts of a historical society—Lesotho—in a critical phase of its experience. What I have to say about anthropology or about jurisprudence can only be said in terms of these particular facts, since they are my sources and my evidence. In thus trying to construct a general argument on the basis of one society's experience—or rather on my experience of one society's experience—I am taking a risk that most anthropologists seem to run: namely, of what Mary Douglas calls 'Bongo-Bongoism' (1970:64). I do not know how this danger can be avoided; I am not even sure that it is worth trying to avoid it anyway, since the only safe way round it would involve either the reduction of anthropology to description, or else (conversely) the abandonment of anthropology for philosophy. The structuralists claim a *via media*; but I have not yet understood their instructions about where to find it, and until I have decoded their messages I feel happier stumbling along my own road, where at least the dangers are familiar ones and the predators are recognisable.

1

Although I cannot really apologise for the 'facts', I recognise that no-one has any duty to share my interest in Lesotho, and I have tried, therefore, to pare the ethnography down to the bone. On the other hand, to satisfy the curiosity which enthusiasts may feel, and indeed to offer some reassurance to all professional readers, I have, in the notes, either provided details in support of any proposition that may seem bare or arbitrary in the text, or slse supplied references to sources where such support may be found. As with any attempt to do neither too little nor too much, there is no way of being sure that one has got it just right. I have no defence against the charge that I have supplied insufficient ethnography any more than that I have offered an excess of it; indeed, both faults could be present at the same time.

My research in Lesotho, on which this book is based, was conducted at various times between 1964 and 1968. A brief account of the territory's earlier history will be found in the opening paragraphs of Chapter 2; in this introduction, I turn to the more modern background and offer a short description of the country as it has developed in recent years and as it is today.[1]

The Kingdom of Lesotho (legally styled 'Basutoland' until independence) is entirely surrounded by the Republic of South Africa. Its total land area is rather under 12,000 square miles (about the size of Belgium), of which the greater part is mountainous. The border lowlands and lower foothills form a crescent round the north and west, extending at one extremity into the Orange River valley (see the map on page 4).

Outside the few semi-urban centres, the economy is based on subsistence cultivation in the lowlands and foothills, and on herding (largely of cattle and goats) in the mountains. The arable land is poor, shallow and deeply eroded by gullies, while the mountain pastures are seriously over-stocked. Extremes of climate range from about 90° F. in the lowlands in the summer to very deep frosts in the winter. Most rainfall occurs in the summer months, between October and April, but it is not so predictable that well-founded fears of drought can be excluded.

The total population probably approaches one million, but of these something in the region of 120,000 are absentee labourers working in South Africa; most of these absentees are men aged between

twenty and forty years—the ablest section of the potential workforce
—and the economic survival of the nation depends largely on their
remittances.

About two-thirds of the population live in the lowland plain, where
nearly all the arable land is found. (Only about 1,450 square miles of
the country is available for arable cultivation, the rest being either
grazing land or mountainous terrain of little or no productive worth.)
The capital, Maseru, with a population of about 7,000, is much the
largest urban area.

Over 99 per cent of the population are Africans, and of these some
85 per cent are Sotho, most of the remaining 15 per cent or so being
of Nguni origin (notably Xhosa). These differences in ethnic affilia-
tion, however, have little importance. They do not in themselves
represent political division of structural significance, nor do they
constitute serious linguistic barriers. There has been no European
settlement in Lesotho.

About two-thirds of the population are enumerated as Christians,
the leading denominations being the Roman Catholic Church and
the Lesotho Evangelical Mission, of French Protestant origin.
Education is widespread, most schools being run by missions. The
main campus of the University of Botswana, Lesotho and Swaziland
is located in Lesotho; it serves all three territories, but most of the
students are local. A national literacy rate of 60 per cent is claimed,
and although this figure must be treated with some caution, Lesotho
nevertheless enjoys one of the highest literacy rates in Africa. It
would be difficult (in the lowlands at any rate) to find any community
without several members who can read and write Sesotho, and a few
with some passable knowledge of English as well.

It was never supposed that Lesotho would remain permanently a
British colony, the expectation being that in due course it would be
incorporated into the Union of South Africa. Until shortly before
the outbreak of the Second World War, only the most minimal
government was attempted, and no effort was made to develop the
country economically or to prepare it for any other destiny than as a
part of the Union. This prospect was resisted, however, even before
the post-war governments of the Union and later the Republic
adopted racial policies that made incorporation totally unacceptable
to the Basotho. Throughout these decades, Lesotho was governed
by the Crown (*viz.*, Secretary of State) acting through the High
Commission in Pretoria. Effective government was in the hands of

the Resident Commissioner and the administrative hierarchy deployed under him.

In 1903, a Basutoland National Council of chiefly composition was convened, which continued for the next forty years to meet on a regular and official basis as a consultative and advisory body for the guidance of the Colony's government. In the middle 1940s, District

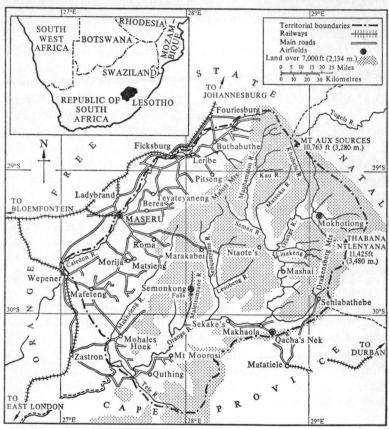

MAP OF SOUTHERN AFRICA AND LESOTHO

Councils were also established, though without much effective power, and a Basutoland National Treasury was set up in 1946. However, it was not until 1960 that any real degree of responsible internal self-government, even on a limited scale, was given to the Basotho—apart, of course, from the chiefly administration of 'native affairs' which, on the pattern of Indirect Rule, were largely left in the hands of the traditional indigenous authorities. Under the new constitution, the National Council had a qualified right to propose legislation on all matters not reserved to the Resident Commissioner, and an Executive Council, not unlike a Cabinet and including Basotho members, was charged with the day-to-day administration. The sovereign government, however, retained overriding powers, including the residual right to veto any proposed legislation and to legislate itself directly in any sphere.

By this time, organised political parties were active in Lesotho. In the early 1960s, political activity was intense, the bitterest opposition being that between the radical Congress Party (BCP) and the moderate MFP, the latter (through its patronage by the Paramount Chief and its popularity with the colonial government) enjoying a virtual monopoly in the Councils, whilst the former enjoyed the greatest degree of support among the people as a whole. These political activities coincided with, and were largely prompted by, the strong movement in favour of independence that captured much of the nation in the early 1960s, and which found expression in the 1963 Report of the Basutoland Constitutional Commission. Following this, a new 'self-government' constitution was inaugurated in 1965. The effect of this was to vest ultimate sovereignty in a bicameral legislature, while recognising the 'special position' of the Paramount Chief. The latter was now given the official title of Motlotlehi, and was to become King of Lesotho with the attainment of independence. The lower house consisted of sixty members, elected by universal adult suffrage. The Senate was composed of the twenty-two principal chiefs *ex-officio* together with eleven other persons nominated by Motlotlehi. Motlotlehi also retained the power to act in accordance with his own judgment in certain other matters, notably land administration. Executive government lay with a Prime Minister and Cabinet responsible to the lower house, the Senate being clothed with certain powers of delay. The first election, to the surprise of many, produced a narrow majority for the very conservative National Party.[2] It was under this government and this constitution that the independent Kingdom of Lesotho came into being in October 1966. It remained in force until January 1970 when it was suspended by the Prime Minister, Chief Leabua Jonathan. The monarchy survived, though in weakened form, while for the rest a Council of Ministers has ruled by decree. A form of nominated parliamentary assembly was restored in 1973.

A note on method[3]

Much of the material on which this study most explicitly rests was drawn from the records of the Basotho courts lodged with the Judicial Commissioner in Maseru. I was able to work through several thousand case-dockets, covering the period from 1944 through to the point at which new cases were coming up for hearing late in 1966. Virtually all the files carried a complete transcription of the original proceedings in Sesotho, comprising a long-hand record of the evidence given in the court of first instance and the complete judgments of the presidents of all the Basotho courts involved. In some cases, English translations were also included, a facility that was especially useful in the earlier months of my work. Some five hundred cases were selected for special attention, and these have provided the bulk of the systematically organised legal material underlying this book. A written transcript of proceedings is kept by all Basotho courts. This is entered in long-hand in interleaved books, the principal being retained by the clerk of court and the carbon duplicate remitted to a superior court in the event of appeal. Evidence once given is read back to the witness, who then signs or places his mark on the record. Whenever I attended court hearings, I found that this procedure was quite attentively observed, and I have no reason to think that my presence was an important factor in this. Literacy in Lesotho is sufficiently widespread for there to be no technical problem in ensuring a complete and accurate Sesotho record. No one would claim that all the records are perfect: but they are good enough to count as reliable material when read in the light of wider and deeper knowledge of Sotho society than the cases themselves directly reveal. Indeed, sometimes their very deficiencies can be instructive.

In general terms, and *mutatis mutandis*, I would adopt a very similar position to that of L. A. Fallers in his own use of Soga court records (1969: 347 ff., Appendix B: 'The Case Records'). I would particularly endorse his conclusion (350):

> [First], the transcripts do have the merit of presenting what the Basoga themselves consider an adequate representation of the trial process. Second, while I was unable to follow up most cases with extra-courtroom investigation, I do have the knowledge that comes from extended fieldwork in Busoga, much of it focused

upon those areas of Soga life relevant to the case material. The institutions that form the social matrix of these disputes were investigated with some care. Without this, of course, the case records would have remained essentially unintelligible.

I would not consider claiming for myself either the quantity or the quality of the fieldwork experience that Fallers displays in his work on Busoga, any more than I would be so presumptuous as to set my own study beside his; but, within these limits, rather similar considerations apply. My 'extra-judicial' fieldwork, moreover, which was mainly spent in a lowland hamlet near the royal village of Matsieng, was directed specifically to those institutions and dimensions of social structure that were most relevant to my legal interests; I do not think I am over-optimistic in believing that the months thus devoted to the study of the 'social matrix' equipped me reasonably well for the task of understanding the law.

The methodology of this study thus departs from the more usual anthropological practice: the micro-analysis of case material in its full interactional setting. In a recent survey of the field, Gulliver (1969a) has convincingly expressed the view that case studies are at the heart of the social anthropology of law, and endorsed Hoebel's call for 'cases, cases and more cases' (quoted in Gulliver 1969a: 13). Of cases, indeed, there are plenty in this book, but most of them do not principally reflect 'the problem focus of research and analysis' as Gulliver sees it—'*the process of dispute settlement*, set in the empirical study of detailed cases' (1969a: 13–14, original italics). My method has been not to use cases as a lawyer might use them in modern society, where the law very largely lives a life and pursues a logic of its own, but nevertheless to use them for the extraction of specifically legal concepts and the study of specifically legal issues. The wider sociology of Sotho social organisation has, in other words, been the starting point rather than the goal of my inquiries. I have not used dispute procedures in order to found an analysis of total processes of social interaction. I have, rather, moved in from a wider sociological field in order to solve some analytical problems about law. I make no particular claim for my own choice of direction in competition with any other. There is still plenty of room for a variety of approaches, and I will be happy enough if my methods have yielded something of profit, and have been appropriate to the inquiry.

Language and orthography[4]

The most generally approved name for the language spoken in
Lesotho is Southern Sotho. In this book, I call it simply 'Sesotho'. I
have adhered throughout to what is usually known as the 'Basutoland orthography', rather than the 1959 Republic of South Africa
orthography, which has not so far been adopted in the territory.
Members of the nation are called 'Mosotho' in the singular and
'Basotho' in the plural. In most other contexts, I use 'Sotho' without
a prefix as a universal adjective.

1 Customary law

Floods of ink have been wasted on debates about the definition of law, of custom, and of 'law and custom'.[1] What follows is not intended as an addition to this very largely metaphysical, or at least terminological, discussion. But some substantive consideration of customary law and customary systems seems justifiable, indeed mandatory, in the light of the preoccupations that mark the present study.

Even the term 'customary systems' raises an initial problem, at least in so far as the word 'system' implies a rigorous, logically ordered and complete array of juristic propositions and normative rules. In the ideal legal 'system', at least, all norms are mutually consistent in themselves and in their implications; there are no gaps in it—no juristic vacuum; and each item can be derived from some other item (a concept or a rule) of higher order. Customary law falls short of all these requirements. The concepts it employs are not rigorously defined; logical ordering exists more by chance than on principles of structure; the scope for deduction is very limited; it is far from being logically complete; and its rules are not always mutually consistent. Professor Stone has suggested (1964) what is implied by referring to legal 'systems', and since customary law does not measure up to his well-argued requirements, some less misleading term for the assemblage of norms and prescriptions that constitute it must be found. Perhaps more consonantly with modern usage it could be called an open set. But to say that customary law is a set of normative rules is trivial, indeed almost truistic. It fails to suggest the specific features that distinguish *customary* law from any other unsystematic set of norms. The special qualities of customary law cannot be purely negative; no satisfactory conception of customary law can be arrived at simply by taking a systematic legal order and eliminating from it in turn its consistency, its conceptual precision,

9

its completeness and its logic and supposing that the residue constitutes customary law.

The word 'customary' itself suggests a more positive approach.
Although the term 'customary' has misleading overtones for English-
speaking lawyers, it has the virtue of bringing out a central characteristic of certain forms of legal order. It deflects attention away from
those who teach or interpret the law, and directs it instead towards
those who live it and use it. Customary law emerges from what
people do, or—more accurately—from what people believe they
ought to do, rather than from what a class of legal specialists consider
they should do or believe. This is not to deny that, in any society,
some people are credited with a more acute sensitivity to such
obligations than others, or even that the incumbents of certain
statuses (defined often by age or seniority) have a *prima facie* claim to
possess this greater sensitivity. Differences in human qualities are
universally recognised, and in hierarchically ordered societies the
senior grades will be assumed to be more, rather than less, generously
endowed with wisdom, understanding and insight than other people.
Yet the ultimate test is not, 'what does this judge say?' but rather
'what do the *participants* in the law regard as the rights and duties
that apply to them?' The real task of the customary jurist is to answer
this last question, not to apply deductive or analytic reasoning to a
set of professionally formulated legal concepts.

Again, the word 'customary' itself points to this conclusion,
suggesting as it does a law that emerges, not from jurisprudential
interpretation, but from the 'customs' in terms of which the actors
themselves determine their actions. However, there are serious
dangers in relying too much on the concept of custom—whether in
its technical or in its everyday sense—for an understanding of
customary law (Hamnett 1971). The first danger arises from the fact
that, at least in the English doctrine, 'custom', if it is to have the
force of law, must have a series of attributes not all of which have any
formal application to the kind of law now under discussion. Thus, it
is said that a custom must be 'reasonable'. But this is usually little
more than an ethnocentrism. The test of 'reasonableness' has a place
only when the authoritative exponents of the law are at a social and
institutional distance from the rest of society. Where they are not set
at this distance, reasonableness and the common social perception
fuse. The test of conformity with statute has, rather obviously, little
or no application in societies where no distinct legislative institutions

exist. The requirement of immemorial antiquity raises more complex problems, which can be considered in conjunction with those posed by the further stipulation that custom must not change. In the first place, English 'custom' of the kind to which these several tests apply, is essentially a particular derogation from or extension of the 'general custom of the realm', *consuetudines regni*. The 'custom' in customary law, on the other hand, itself constitutes the law, and is in no way an island of privilege or exemption that prescinds from or adds to a more general rule.[2] This does not, of course, mean that one homogeneous body of custom necessarily pervades the whole of society; indeed, nothing is more characteristic of customary law than its particularism and localisation. It means only that any customary norm is, at its own level, the juristic equal of any other and does not have, as it were, to be 'proved against' some other norm which is otherwise presumed to apply. English custom, then, is necessarily derogative; it is an exception to a general rule, and is consequently intrinsically particular and specialised. The tests of antiquity and unchanging continuity, therefore, make sense since they can be taken to justify, juridically, the exceptional case. The most important norms of customary law, on the other hand, are usually quite different in character. *Though they are concrete, they are general.* Customary law is pre-eminently embodied in a set of concrete principles, the detailed application of which to particular cases is flexible and subject to change (Allott 1960: ch. 3.) The principle is unchanging, no doubt, but it is not always an easy matter to determine when any given norm or rule is an authentic principle or is nothing more than the practical application of a general norm to a particular case. If, therefore, custom is to be described as stable or immutable or unchanging, this permanency must be attributed only to the most general norms and not to the subordinate or contingent norms that emerge when a given principle is applied in a concrete case.[3] These subordinate norms can, should and do change, in response to varying social situations. Moreover, when a general rule is applied in a concrete case, the law is not, as it is in systems that recognise the binding precedent, thereby made more specific or narrow. When the case is concluded, the law returns, as it were, from its brief excursion into detail and reverts to its normal condition of generality.

A further stipulation found in modern systems of law is that custom must be observed as of right. This requirement is different in kind from the other rules, and is in principle fully applicable to customary law, indeed it is crucial to any analysis. Besides the misunderstandings to which the technical lawyer is liable, and which have just been discussed, there is a further danger of an opposite kind, namely that custom may be interpreted to mean no more than *practice*. If law is to be looked for not in those who expound it as professionals but in those who live it and use it, it could be supposed that it can be found simply by looking at what people do—law becomes simply a function of practice. No misunderstanding could be more complete. To make practice the formal source of law in the customary field is to be untrue to the facts, where people recognise in normative law a moral authority, a legitimacy, that they do not accord to practice or usage as a whole. No approach to customary law that fails to take this indigenous recognition into account can ever be satisfactory. The certainty of this distinction is not affected by the difficulty of drawing a precise line of demarcation. People may not be sure whether certain intermediate norms are authoritative or not, but they may still be clear that X is in a real sense 'law' while Y is definitely 'not law' (cf. Schapera 1955: 37–8). This is all that is necessary in order to make the point. Moreover, norms can never be equated with practice since so much of practice is contrary to the norms. Customary law does not say that a man should not steal his neighbour's chickens more than occasionally, or graze his cattle on another man's fields more than anybody else does. It says that these things may not be done at all. For these reasons, the test of observance as a right, if interpreted as an affirmation of the authoritative and regulatory character of normative rules, is a critical feature of customary as of any other law.[4]

Another way of putting this would perhaps be to say that practice is not, and cannot be, the *formal* source of customary law. It remains, of course, its *material* source, in that customary law is materially abstracted or derived from practice, rather than by a series of logical operations upon a legal formula or proposition. It is not just that the *original* rule of common law was derived from practice, but was then made the object of jurisprudential operations in the course of its later development. In customary law, not only the original but also the derived norms are related to those who *participate*—to the actors in the social situation—and not only to a professional body of specialised teachers and judges.

The phrase 'actors in the social situation' points to the last formal characteristic of customary law to be discussed: its social origin and character. This might seem an obvious feature of all law, and hardly worth insisting upon. However, if the ultimate test of customary law is not 'what does the judge say?' but 'what do the participants regard as the rule?' the question arises of the eccentric participant or actor who regards as a *rule* some private and personal predilection of his own. If customary law derives from practices that are endowed with authority by the practitioners, how is it possible to deal (analytically) with idiosyncratic practitioners? It is to close this gap that it becomes necessary to stress the social character of customary law. The argument here is not that a total 'society'—whatever that may be—defines one homogeneous law by derivation from universally sanctioned practice; though in fact this meets the case in certain instances, it would be much too rigorous an assumption for most non-literate societies. To say that law is social and not individual is not to imply that between the individual and the total society to which he belongs there are no intermediate social groups whose corporate and semi-independent character validates their own local law. Clans, sub-clans, lineages and even individual families can constitute social groups in this sense, in such a way that the norms to which they attribute authority are socially and not merely individually legitimised. The exact nature of the groups that possess this, so to speak, 'public' character will vary from society to society. Moreover, the domain within which this public character exists will vary according to the kind of rule or subject matter involved. Thus, as in Sotho law, questions of inheritance may be determinable by the immediate agnatic kinsmen of the deceased, while questions of succession to office may be determined by some more widely defined group, and questions of land-tenure may be referred to some other authority again. So variations may be expected not only from society to society, but also, within any one society, from one type of case or subject-matter to another. The essential fact is that the law is always socially defined. In no known society is it open to each individual to find his own law. The legitimacy, the imputed authority with which customary law is clothed, is not transmitted by a legislative assembly or a specialist judge, but neither is it the product of an individual's idiosyncrasy.

II

The argument so far has raised a number of substantive and not merely definitional issues and suggests a formula that omits purely contingent and accidental features and yet is not entirely trivial. *Customary law can be regarded as a set of norms which the actors in a social situation abstract from practice and which they invest with binding authority.* The positive content of this definition may be taken as fourfold: the relation of norms to *practice* rather than to 'lawyers' reasoning'; the dominant role of the *actors* or participants in the determination of law; the *authoritative* or legitimate, rather than merely factual or utilitarian, character of the emergent rules; and the essentially *social* nature of their validation and status. But it is equally important to be clear about what this formulation does not say—the questions that it still leaves open. An examination of these absences will indicate some further important features of customary law.

In the first place, the formula proposed leaves room for those who act unlawfully. The typical unlawful act is one which the actor knows to be wrong, rather than one performed by an actor who acts on a different set of normative assumptions. In the customary context this tends to mean something rather more than that the actor knows his act to be in a simple objective sense 'against the law'; rather, he will himself share the general social evaluation of his act, while hoping that he will 'get away' with it. But, and this is the second point, this does not, naturally enough, rule out the existence of different and conflicting interpretations of the law. No doubt this will always be the case, in all legal systems; but in customary law, the point needs to be stressed, not only because a misreading of the argument about law and society might suggest that conflict and disagreement were eliminated, but also because the specific character of customary norms has a direct bearing on the scope for disputed interpretation. Reference has already been made to the fact that the fundamental norms of customary law tend to take the form of *general but at the same time concrete principles*, and it was stressed that the effect of a particular application of the norm is not to give added precision or specificity to the law in future cases; rather, the law reverts to its, as it were, 'normal' condition of generality when it has accomplished its mission in the particular case in hand. This is one major reason why disputes over the proper interpretation of rules are a constant possibility. It is reinforced by the fact that, analytically considered, the norms of customary law often seem mutually inconsistent. This inconsistency arises from the fact that legal rules are not considered in the abstract but in the context of different social situations. It is only if the analyst insists upon following all the logical implications of each of two analytically inconsistent norms that their conflict becomes inevitable, and the trained lawyer is tempted to take the view that one of them must triumph and the other perish, or at least that some boundary (whether procedural or logical) must be drawn to demarcate for each its area of competency or relevance. If on the other hand the general and concrete principle returns to generality after each application, it can coexist with other principles without either being sacrificed to the other. At the same time, in particular cases, the two can conflict and provide each of the parties to a dispute with an armoury of legal arguments.

Nor does the formulation suggested above ignore the fact that some people may be regarded as more authoritative exponents of the law than others. The incumbents of certain positions, typically the hereditary position of chief, may be especially privileged in this regard. It is true that it has not been a feature of lawful chieftainship in Lesotho that chiefs were despots or tyrants; Moshoeshoe was very different from Chaka, not only in personality but in the character of his office and in his political and historical situation. When a Sotho chief gave judgment, it used to be said '*ho lumile*' ('it has thundered'); but the despotical implications of this saying are contradicted by a still more celebrated and ideologically fundamental maxim, that 'a chief is a chief by the people' ('*morena ke morena ka batho*'). Yet too much can be made of the 'essentially democratic' character of traditional monarchy. To stress the social and in a certain sense 'popular' character of customary law, in chiefly societies as in others, is certainly to recall something of what is implied in the American term 'folk-ways'; but this does not exclude the indubitable truth, neatly expressed by Professor Goebel, that a folk-way may be the way of the folk in power (quoted in Plucknett 1949: 7). This indeed is one of the crucial ambiguities of domination (in the sense of *Herrschaft*, Weber 1947: part 3; 1954: 322–48). A hereditary chieftainship develops its own interests as an ascriptive status-group, which are analytically (and can become empirically) separate from those of the community. Where chieftainship is *itself* a central political value in the society, the ambiguities of its domination grow to create a broad area of 'indeterminacy', and it is precisely here that 'force' is mediated to 'law' (or 'power' to 'authority', in terms of an alternative and overlapping scheme, Smith 1960).

An empirical feature of most customary law is that it is unwritten. This is more than a simple descriptive fact, for it has implications for the *kind* of law that emerges.[5] When law is written, it is possible to isolate it from its social context and to seal it off in books; jurisprudential analysis can then begin. The fact that customary law is unwritten is one reason why it remains both general and concrete. It remains *general* because its detailed applications in different places are not made known to all, only the principle being universally remembered, and *concrete* because detailed logical analysis is impracticable when the analyst has got no accurate and objective reports on which to rely. The doctrine of precedent is hard to set up when there is no written record of earlier decisions. This allows customary norms to be flexible and adaptable, and to function, in Plucknett's words, as 'instruments for legal change rather than the fossilised remnants of a dead past' (1949: 7). But it is not just a matter of saying that pre-literate societies lack certain cultural techniques and that therefore their law is what it is. It is hardly too much of a paradox to reverse the order of cause and effect and assert that the unwritten character of customary law is the product or effect of its general nature, rather than the reverse. Max Weber has shown (1947) how essential writing is for the functioning of a modern rational bureaucratic system. But the relevant point in the present context is that it is not the mere fact of writing but the use to which it is put that is crucial. In Lesotho, it happens to be the fact that written records of the proceedings and judgments of most courts and tribunals are kept, but this is not enough to constitute a 'written law', since the records are not, on the whole, then used as a basis for analysis, the establishment of precedent, or the abstract manipulation of concepts. At least until very recently, writing might as well not exist for all the part that it has played in the shaping of the law.

This general view of customary law may be compared with the approaches adopted by Max Gluckman in his classic studies of the Barotse (1955, 1965, etc.) and by L. A. Fallers in his work on the Basoga (1965, 1969, etc.).

The most rigorous definition of law among the Barotse offered by Gluckman states that 'Lozi have law as a set of rules accepted by all normal members of the society as defining right and reasonable ways in which persons ought to behave in relation to each other and to things, including ways of obtaining protection for one's rights' (1955: 229, italics omitted). Elsewhere, he describes it as 'the body of rules, the *corpus juris*, on which judges draw to give a decision . . . and as *adjudication*, a process by which cases are tried and judgments or *legal rulings* given' (226 f. original italics). The emphasis on rules in these formulations implies what is in other passages made explicit, that for Gluckman law in Lozi society is a specific and irreducible social fact; it is indeed a matter for direct ethnographic observation —'empirically *law* . . . influences the behaviour of both Lozi judges and public' (1955: 352, original italics). 'Law as such will be distinguished by observers, and distinguished by the people, from other types of social fact' (265). He proposes (230 f.) the term 'alegal' as a way of describing other societies, such as the Nuer, that to varying degrees lack 'law' in this sense; this neologism, he suggests, makes it possible to assert the relative absence of *law* in such societies without seeming to attribute to them any necessary 'lawlessness' or 'illegality'.

Gluckman stresses that Lozi litigants and witnesses work with the same legal and moral norms as do the judges (1955:49). This does not, however, mean that the courts regard it as superfluous to spell out these rules and also to reiterate the more basic norms of which particular rules are the concrete expression. 'Large parts of the judgments read like sermons' (45), but the purpose of such judicial utterances is not really homiletic. Gluckman lays stress on the generality, flexibility and unspecific character of Lozi rules of law, and argues that 'in different cases different rules can be selected for enforcement' (1955: 283; and cf. 1965: 17). The judicial utterance serves to indicate the selection that is tacitly made, and so to legitimate the decision. Different laws, Gluckman points out, can be stated separately with certainty. When they are combined, in application to particular situations, various laws are given different weight (1955: 202). Ambiguity, vagueness and generality are seen as having judicial value, words which are most fundamental and important tending indeed to be the least precise (1955: 295). These features 'allow the judges to manipulate the concepts themselves in order to give decisions in accordance with their ideas of law and justice. . . . The certainty of the law is maintained through what is clearly chanciness in litigation' (1955: 305, 310). 'Most judgments . . . seem

to show that a judge decides on the merits of the case and then
works out a legal argument to defend his decision' (1955: 276).[6]

Much of this analysis is reflected in the view of Sotho law adopted
in the present study, so it is perhaps all the more important that one
point of theoretical divergence also should be made clear. Gluckman
sometimes speaks of the exercise of judicial 'discretion' in the making
of a selection among the various rules and in the assignation of
different weightings to them (e.g., 1955: 202, 234). Much of the
present study will be concerned with a rejection of the notion of
'discretion' in this sort of context, suggestive as it is of a polarity
between rule-governed (sc., judicial) behaviour on the one hand and
power-based (sc., political) activity on the other. Gluckman is of
course wholly right in his view of the rules of law permitting a
variety of outcomes as a consequence of their flexibility and lack of
precision; and at one level he is also obviously correct in saying of
Lozi judges (as indeed of judges anywhere) that they construct their
judgments or opinions after the event, as a way of legally justifying
the conclusion they have arrived at. But there are better ways of
dealing with these issues than by speaking of a 'discretion'.
Gluckman's own striking phrase about the certainty of the law being
maintained through the chanciness of litigation puts the emphasis
more squarely where it belongs. The whole process is one of law.
This does not mean that decisions are constrained; but neither does
this absence of constraint imply that an exercise of 'discretion' is
involved, at least if that term includes the idea of non-legal or
'political' modes of decision-making (see also below, pp. 78f. and
113f.).

Fallers's analysis of Soga law has already been referred to, and
other aspects of it are fully considered in a later chapter (pp. 107ff.)
Borrowing the notion of 'categorizing concepts' from Levi (1948),
Fallers notes that 'by means of such concepts, judges . . . order the
cases that come before them. . . . They are the tools of "moral
over-simplification", of issue narrowing. . . . By means of them, the
almost infinite complexity of circumstances surrounding a particular
case may be reduced . . . to problems of inclusion and exclusion.'
This is the test of law for Fallers, and it enables him to say that 'the
tribunals of the Basoga are . . . true "courts of law" because they
reason legally, with categorising concepts that narrow and frame the
issues for decision; but . . . their legal reasoning is both relatively
implicit . . . and relatively concrete' (Fallers 1969: 20f.; and cf. 32).[7]

Soga material, he claims, 'shows how legal a system can be without overt communication about the application of legal concepts— without precedent or legislation. . . . What, then, are some of the distinguishing features of law without precedent, Soga style? It is . . . popular . . . accessible . . . implicit . . .' (1969: 312–14). The 'implicit' quality of Soga norms seems to be more evident than that of either the Lozi or the Sotho, but the lack of precedent relates closely to what has been argued above—that a decision in one case does not (as it does in precedent-governed systems) narrow or *specify* the rule in its future applications. After each excursion, so to speak, into particular cases, the law reverts to the generality that marks it when it is 'at rest'. 'Each sitting represents a fresh start' (Fallers 1969: 312). This is an aspect of the particular kind of *inconsistency* that has been noted before, and it helps to show how this inconsistency works, and is indeed serviceable. Gluckman refers to it among the Lozi: 'This inconsistency in judgments in individual disputes . . . does not alter the substantive body of law and legal principles. Their application varies: they remain unchanged' (1955: 282).

III

Gluckman and Fallers, of course, have studied African societies which, like that of the Sotho, are kingdoms or chieftaincies. A comparative glance at legal procedures in an acephalous society will help to bring out some further points, both about customary law in general and about the characteristics of 'chiefly' law in particular. P. H. Gulliver's admirable study of the Arusha (1963) provides an excellent starting-point for such an inquiry. Gulliver shows how dispute settlement among the Arusha depends upon a series of direct or sometimes mediated confrontations at various levels of formality between the disputing parties or their spokesmen, counsellors or supporters. The principal goal of the procedures is to restore the social peace, rather than to impose on a reluctant defendant a set of obligations (to compensate, to repay a debt, to fulfil an undertaking) derived from an abstract calculation of universal liabilities. The whole process of settlement is set within a framework of normative rules, which define the presuppositions of the parties and draw the contours of their mutual expectations. But no subordinate agent or agency dictates the emergent compromise, or even plays a major role in arriving at it. The procedure is essentially one

of mutual adjustment, and it is of course this aspect of affairs that
gives the settlement its stability and strength, Imposed settlements
by their nature lead to resentment on the part of the unsuccessful
litigant; mutual agreement implies equal acceptance of the result.
It is, in fact, seen as a breakdown of the traditional and proper
procedures if the parties have recourse to the modern magistrates'
courts, where judicial settlements may in the last resort have to be
imposed upon them, to the lasting dissatisfaction of either or both.

Gulliver contrasts Arusha settlement procedure with the processes
of other societies, especially with those that have superordinate
chiefs or other more specialised judicial officers. Although his
terminology differs from that which Smith (1960) adapts from Weber,
the trend of thought is the same. He attaches particular importance
to the presence or absence of a superordinate officer such as a chief or
a judge, arguing that in the absence of such a person the 'political'
element will play an important part in arriving at a settlement. On
the other hand, where a superordinate judge exists, the 'political'
element is present only as an abuse, and because of the weakness and
fallibility of mortal men; ideally, where a presiding officer super-
intends the court or moot, the 'political' element disappears and only
the 'judicial' function remains. Gulliver proposes a continuous scale
from 'judicial' to 'political', and very reasonably places the Arusha
towards the 'political' end of the continuum (1963: 301).

> The resolution of the matter is not a case of reaching a decision
> as to which disputant is supported by the norms and to what
> extent. . . . These processes and inter-party struggles can only be
> understood in terms of the social system in which the participants
> are involved in ordinary social life.

This is a very fair way of putting it, and there is no reason to
quarrel with Gulliver about the position at which the Arusha should
be placed within this framework. But the framework itself is inade-
quate in several respects.[8]

In the first place, the implied comparison is not being drawn
between equivalent levels of structure.[9] Arusha settlements should
not be compared with the judicial process in Lozi (Gluckman 1955;
1965), far less with English society, but with extra-judicial or pre-
judicial settlements, which account for the overwhelming majority
of 'litigable' disputes. Much of what is said of the Arusha could,
mutatis mutandis, be said of the 90 per cent of disputes in contempor-

ary Britain that are settled out of court or before reaching the courts at all.

Of course, it is true that in Britain these settlements are reached under the shadow, as it were, of the courts; the parties or their solicitors know that the courts are there, and this knowledge influences their conduct in working towards a settlement. But this only introduces a second complaint against Gulliver's account, which is that he undervalues the normative element in the Arusha settlement process. He is, though, a meticulous enough ethnographer to provide evidence of this himself, and this is why in the above account of his findings, mention was made of the framework of norms in which the settlement procedure is set, defining the moral presuppositions and mutual expectations of the parties. In a relatively homogeneous society, these norms and expectations do not need authoritative exposition by formal courts. But none of the evidence cited makes sense unless it is seen in the context of a normative system overarching the 'political' process of compromise and negotiation and injecting into it a standard of what is, in fact, to be regarded as a reasonable rather than a leonine settlement. These norms (as Gulliver says) do of course arise from (though they are not reducible to) 'the social system in which the participants are involved in ordinary social life'; but they are none the less real for not being articulated through specialised judicial institutions.

Third, it is misleading to analyse the role of the superordinate judge in the way Gulliver implies. He suggests that the introduction of a 'judge' so to speak, converts the process from being a largely 'political' into an ideally 'judicial' one: any 'political' element now present being the result, as it were, of the inevitable imperfections of humankind.[10] He accounts for the differences between Arusha and Lozi settlement processes largely on these grounds. This is to make too much of the judge's role and at the same time to say too little about it. Quite as important as the presence or absence of a 'judge' is the question of whether he is or is not a *specialised* judicial officer. In most traditional chiefly societies, men were not appointed to be judges: what we analyse out as their judicial function was part of the ascriptive status of chieftainship. A chief has to make many decisions, some of which we may legitimately characterise as 'judicial', but this analytical distinction may have no empirical counterpart in terms of the social perception of the chief's role.[11]

It is contended here that where judicial office is only an analytically separable aspect of a role which empirically comprises a variety of other functions, the persistence of certain 'political' features is not to be regarded as a sign of human fallibility but as a structural corollary of the office. It is, in fact, a perfectly *legitimate* element in chiefly decision-making, where differentiation has not reached a point at which specialised judges are appointed to carry out specifically judicial tasks. But this does *not* mean that the 'political' element falls outside the area of normative control. This assertion constitutes one of the central themes of the present study, and will be echoed in the chapters that follow as well as re-subjected to a closer analysis in the conclusion. It involves the concept of what may be called 'executive law'—a category of legal action that is not simply reducible to 'political' and 'judicial' components. Executive law is the characteristic *legality* of chieftainship. This approach has implications that underline what has been argued in an earlier passage: that there is what may be called a 'specificity' about law and legal action that is only obscured by an over-insistence on the notion of 'social control'. It has been remarked that there is an inherent ambivalence in chiefly *Herrschaft*, and as a consequence of this there is little point in debating in the abstract whether the putting down of an overmighty subject is the maintenance of a legitimate order or the self-interested defence of privilege (or both). Empirically and extrinsically the two cases are exactly the same, whereas legitimacy lies in the eye of the beholder—or, more exactly, of the actor. The deficiency of the concept of social control is that it stops short at this empirical and extrinsic identity and obscures the 'specificity of law' by distracting attention away from the normative element that discriminates legality from coercion. It is no accident that the vogue for 'social control' coincided with the continued if disguised dominance of positivism in social anthropology. Malinowski was rather too glib in his repudiation not only of 'codes, courts and constables' (1926) but of the 'cake of custom' too. The rather commonsensical account that tends to emerge from his work is only slightly less improbable than the legalisms and automatisms that he attacked. Much of the trouble here arises, as has been suggested, from the word 'custom' and its derivatives (customary, accustom, etc.), where the ambiguities have the effect of obliterating the distinction between 'fact' and 'norm'; and of course it is precisely this obliteration that has recommended the word to generations of positivists. But the solution to this theoretical problem is not to polarise 'customary' or 'executive' law into the analytical dichotomies of 'judicial' and 'political'. Executive law is *law* (however open its practitioners may be to the subversions of power) just as the specialised 'judicial' law of modern societies is law (however open it may be to the subversions of analytical logic). The analyst's task is to describe its operations, and to relate them to the structural features of the societies that characteristically generate it.

In the following chapters, three particular areas of Sotho law are singled out and examined for the light that they throw on the character and mode of operation of customary law. First of all, the 'public' law of chieftainship succession is shown to involve two distinct principles, here called 'retrospective' and 'circumspective', whose interplay gives rise to the ambiguous system which empirically confronts the observer on the ground. Second, we look at the law governing 'private' succession and inheritance, where rights and claims to rights, and indeed the concept of ownership itself, are seen to share a similar kind of ambiguity, arising from the tension between the general yet concrete norms that control the situation of widows and heirs in the legal arena. Third, the law of land use and occupancy is examined, and here perhaps the simplest and most transparent case is found of the manner in which norms that in a formal sense are incompatible with each other come together to produce a concrete situation of legitimised rights. In all these instances, the notions of law, legitimacy and right can be seen to penetrate and inform the resolution of situations whose outcome, before the event, is uncertain, ambiguous and recalcitrant to purely logical or deductive determination. But, though elements of 'politics' and 'power' clearly play their part in these as in nearly all social actions and transactions, what we are witnessing here is, essentially and above all, the operation of executive *law*.

2   The public law of chieftainship succession[1]

The Sotho nation[2] can be said to take its origin in the early part of the nineteenth century, during and after the Difaqane wars, when the Zulu King Chaka was expanding his kingdom by conquest and destroying, subjugating or scattering before him the greater part of the neighbouring African peoples. Among the smaller groups threatened by the wave of destruction and panic were the Mokoteli sub-clan of the Koena, one of the senior clans of the Sotho-speaking peoples of South Africa. The leadership of the Mokoteli passed into the hands of Moshoeshoe, or Moshesh as he is often called, who established a redoubt on the top of the small mountain of Thaba Bosiu, where he and his warriors managed to maintain themselves until relative peace returned. By 1831, Moshoeshoe had become the acknowledged leader of what was to be the Sotho nation, and founded the lineage from which the ruling chieftainship of Lesotho springs.

For another thirty years, however, Moshoeshoe and his followers had to defend themselves and the territory over which they claimed control against the new threat of the Boer *Voortrekkers*, who were moving north from the Cape towards and beyond the Vaal River, and beginning to settle in the fertile plain of the Orange Valley as they passed. By the time that the legal frontiers of Basutoland were eventually defined at the convention of Aliwal North in 1869, the Basotho people had lost the greater part of the plain running north and west from Maseru and Mafeteng to Thaba Nchu, a rich farming country that now forms part of the *platteland* of the Orange Free State. Moshoeshoe and his people were left with a rectangular slab of South Africa, most of which consists of mountain and high upland plateaus. The upper reaches of the Orange River Valley, and a narrow crescent-shaped plain following the Caledon river round the north-western borders, constitute practically all the arable acreage in Lesotho. When these boundaries were fixed, Basutoland had been for

24

about four years British territory, and its people British subjects, and so both it and they remained until independence was achieved in 1966. (An exception to this was a period of thirteen years from 1871. During these years, Basutoland was attached to Cape Colony, which had recently been granted responsible government; but after the so-called Gun wars, provoked by the Cape Government's attempt to enforce a ban against firearms on the Basotho, the territory was finally brought under the direct rule of the Queen on 12 March 1884, in response to a petition from the chiefs themselves.)

The ruling dynasty founded by Moshoeshoe, and the subordinate chieftainship agnatically linked to it, are known simply as 'Koena' in Lesotho, the narrower term 'Mokoteli' being irrelevant for most internal purposes. Only about one-third of the inhabitants of the territorial nation, however, are members of the Koena people,[3] most of the rest belonging either to other Sotho groups (such as the Phuthi or the Khoakhoa) or to non-Sotho peoples of Nguni origin. An initial problem is to explain the political means whereby the Koena lineages established their hegemonic position. In their advance to supremacy, the Koena chiefs made use of two principal devices. One was intermarriage; the other was what has become known as the institution of 'placing'. The second is the more important, being logically prior to the first as well as more direct in its structural consequences for chiefly leadership. Basically, 'placing' means simply 'appointment' and it refers to the system whereby Moshoeshoe and his successors and senior subordinates appointed members of their own agnatic kin to chieftainship positions over local groups within their territorial control. In the formative decades of Lesotho's history, this meant primarily the placing of Moshoeshoe's closer agnates over more and more areas, any pre-existing authorities being extruded or demoted in the process. In many parts of Lesotho, non-Koena headmen or minor chiefs are to be found, whose grandfathers or great-grandfathers had been independent or largely autonomous chiefs of local communities, some of considerable size. Most of these, over the greater part of Lesotho, have now been reduced to subordinate status and many have ceased to belong to the chieftainship altogether.[4] Only in a few cases do non-Koena chiefs retain major status within the nation, and these have succeeded in keeping hold of their autonomy only by accommodating themselves to the national hegemony achieved by the Koena monarchy.

These exceptional cases apart, the political structure of Lesotho can be mapped fairly accurately on to the genealogical structure of the house of Moshoeshoe. Figure 1 illustrates the first two generations of descent from Moshoeshoe's father, Mokhachane; the entries in lower case on the bottom line show the jurisdictional areas, or 'wards', associated with each patrilineal segment. Although Moshoeshoe appears as only one, albeit the most senior, of the three sons of Mokhachane recorded here, the wards associated with the

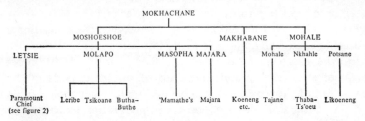

FIGURE 1   *The genealogical distribution of the wards held by the sons of Mokhachane (the bottom line, in lower case, shows the wards associated with the lineage above them)*

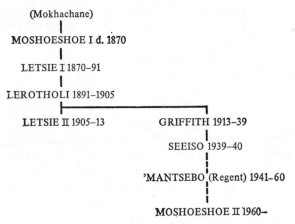

FIGURE 2   *The succession of Paramount Chiefs from Moshoeshoe I to the present day*

Note: 'Mantsebo was Seeiso's senior widow, and bore no male issue. Moshoeshoe II is the eldest son in Seeiso's second house. Griffith was Letsie II's junior brother. All other Paramount Chiefs were the sons of their immediate predecessors.

Makhabane and Mohale lines have been effectively incorporated within one or other of the four sub-dynasties (Letsie, Molapo, Masopha and Majara) originating in Moshoeshoe, the root of the present Koena chieftainship. Moshoeshoe was succeeded by his senior son Letsie I; figure 2 shows the succession of the Paramount Chiefs (as they are known) from the founder to the present day. It will be seen that Letsie II, Lerotholi's senior son, was succeeded by his brother, Griffith.[5] Figure 3 narrows the focus of inquiry to the line of Paramount Chiefs, and illustrates how each succeeding Paramount alienated a part of his direct jurisdiction to junior sons, passing on an ever decreasing area to his own successor as Paramount. (The present King (Paramount Chief), Moshoeshoe II, has in fact no wards directly within his own jurisdiction, having been obliged to

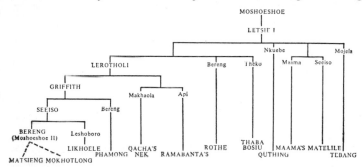

FIGURE 3 *The genealogical distribution of the principal wards held by the sons of Letsie*

convert both Matsieng and Mokhotlong into full wards under their own Principal Chiefs.) Similar processes can be traced for the houses stemming from Moshoeshoe's other sons. It will be seen from figure 3 that, of the twenty-two major chieftainships in Lesotho, no fewer than twelve are within the house of Letsie I. Of the remaining ten, figure 1 shows that five derive from one or other of the other three sons of Moshoeshoe. Only two Principal Chiefdoms and one other major ward remain under non-Koena chiefs.[6]

It will be convenient to signalise the special position of the lines of descent originating in Moshoeshoe's own sons by referring to them as 'cardinal lines'. If the smallest of the four, that of Majara, is left out of account, the indigenous political structure of Lesotho can be said still to reflect the relationship embodied in these cardinal lines. This relationship, however, and its reflection in the subsequent development of Lesotho chieftainship after Moshoeshoe's death, are profoundly ambiguous, and it is the nature and consequences of this ambiguity that must now be explored. A structure like that of the Koena chieftainship can, as a first approximation, be approached in either of two ways. From one point of view, the dynastic relationships established by Moshoeshoe in his sons can be regarded as set up *once and for all*, in such a way that each father lives on, so to speak, in the person of his son. The four cardinal lines move forward in parallel lines from generation to generation, never losing their structural relationship to each other or their relative position within the hierarchy. The point of view that stresses this approach, looking backwards to Moshoeshoe and regarding the arrangements that he made as a wholly unique constitutive act, will be called 'retrospective'. This can be contrasted with an alternative and ultimately incompatible view, in which each successive Paramount Chief, and *mutatis mutandis* each lesser chief too, becomes in his turn a 'new Moshoeshoe', and can do again and on the same pattern what the father of the dynasty did before him. This means not so much looking back at the once-for-all establishment of the cardinal lines by Moshoeshoe as 'looking round' to examine the present order of seniority by reference to the Paramount Chief of the day; for this reason, such an approach can conveniently be called 'circumspective'. Most of the rest of this chapter will be devoted to a closer examination of the distinction between the 'retrospective' and the 'circumspective' models (for that is what they are) of chieftainship seniority, and to tracing the empirical and ideological consequences of their interplay.

Let us begin by giving closer attention to what is involved in the retrospective view. If the relative ranking of cardinal lines is strictly maintained with the passing of generations, the house of Molapo (Moshoeshoe's second son, see figure 1) will always rank second only to the house of Letsie (the Paramount line). This means that the head of the house of Molapo for the time being will rank as the second chief in Lesotho. Similarly, the head of the house of Masopha will rank third, and that of Majara fourth. Figure 4 gives a formal diagrammatic representation of how seniority could be reckoned by the application of the retrospective principle. (The numbers 1 to 8 on the bottom row indicate descending order of seniority.) After the heads of the cardinal lines have been accounted for, junior members of each line are then ranked in terms of the same principles. The most senior immediate agnate of the Paramount Chief, therefore, would rank *after* the heads of the other cardinal lines. His mere agnatic proximity to the royal house would not suffice to displace the cardinal chiefs from the positions which they inherited intact from their establishment by Moshoeshoe. It is implied in the retrospective reckoning of seniority that Moshoeshoe's sons stand as the founding fathers of a lineage structure that has a once-and-for-all character. It is essentially *non-repetitive*, in the sense that it is not open to each succeeding Paramount Chief to start the process afresh by promoting his own sons, and so in effect narrowing the Moshoeshoe lineage by reducing it to its own senior segment.

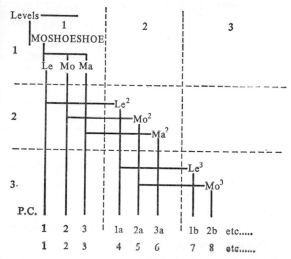

FIGURE 4   *The retrospective model*

However, a problem presents itself within the logic of the retrospective system itself. This arises from the internal segmentation within each of the cardinal lineages, as they divide into subordinate lineages nested within the major lineage that generates them. In other words, there is the problem of what to do with junior sons. Ideally and in principle, this perennial problem was tackled in Lesotho by the placing of junior sons in positions ('caretakings') subordinate to that of the senior son-and-heir. This could mean either that a junior son (or other agnate) was placed in a ward jurisdictionally subordinate to the caretaking normally consigned to the senior son, or that the junior son was given a smaller ward outside the elder brother's caretaking but within the major ward to which the future chief would succeed on his father's death. Various other factors enter into the causes and consequences of the placing of junior sons, and some others of these will be considered shortly. What emerges in the present connection is that although the retrospective system is, as we have seen, non-repetitive at one level, it is repetitive at another. At the level of the cardinal lines, each line retains the seniority which it derives from its relationship to Moshoeshoe, who set up once and for all the cardinal lineages that persist through time in an unchanging structural relationship. But within each cardinal line, secondary and tertiary segmentations occur, on the model of Moshoeshoe and his sons, so that in the next generation the system repeats itself at a lower level of political structure. This segmentation is in its turn in principle non-repetitive at its own level, though in the next generation a similar segmentation and repetition occur at the structural level next below. Each level is thus both a grade in the political hierarchy and a generation in time. These levels are represented along separate dimensions in figure 4. The point to note, however, is that these internal repetitions of the original political process inaugurated, so to speak, by Moshoeshoe cannot—in the retrospective model—have any effect on the ranking of chiefs at any *higher* level of political structure. Above all, the cardinal lines remain intact.

Now, political authority in Lesotho is, in principle, territorial. The Paramount Chief has authority over the whole country, a Principal Chief over the whole of his principal ward, a minor chief over the whole of his minor ward, and so forth; the wards, or jurisdictions, are nested inside one another from lowest to highest, like a set of Chinese boxes. (There is a certain looseness of fit, since a chief at any level of the hierarchy retains a certain amount of his area directly in his own hands, the rest being under the jurisdiction of the chiefs immediately subordinate to him.[7]) The system is very close to what Gluckman has analysed as 'estates of holding' for the Lozi (Gluckman 1943). In terms of the retrospective system, therefore, any chief's position in the genealogical structure should indicate his social ranking and his place in the political hierarchy, including his territorial area and his relationship to the chiefs above and below him. For instance, in figure 4, the chief represented by 2b would hold a minor ward within the major ward of 2a, who in turn would hold his ward within the principal ward 2, which in its turn would be held directly from the Paramount Chief. As we have seen, this pattern is broadly true of the upper levels of the chiefly hierarchy; the genealogical or dynastic system and the system of political and territorial jurisdiction reflect each other almost like mirror images. But at lower levels, the two systems diverge; and even at the highest level, there is real ambiguity in the relationship that is taken to hold between the Paramountcy on the one hand and the other cardinal lines on the other. From a 'pure' retrospectivist position, this failure of the two systems to mirror each other perfectly can be explained as a 'distortion' to be accounted for by the contingencies of history and politics. Let us therefore continue to consider the case retrospectively, and try to identify the source and nature of the 'distortion' in the cases where it occurs.

We have already noticed the recurrence in Lesotho of the perennial problem of what to do with junior sons, and we saw how the problem was provisionally resolved by creating new wards and jurisdictions within and subordinate to existing chieftainships. In the earlier stages of Koena expansion, this process coincided with the political object of extruding or demoting non-Koena chiefs; for it must be stressed that the 'placing' of a chief in a newly created jurisdiction has a politically debilitating effect on all the chiefs now subordinate to him. Not only is a further link introduced into the chain of command between subject and Principal Chief, but the newly placed chief requires lands and jurisdiction for his support, and these can only come from his new subordinates. This political, economic and jurisdictional depression of non-Koena chiefs was, of course, a point in its favour in the eyes of the ruling dynasty, and as we have already seen it was one of the principal ways in which the Koena lineage achieved its political pre eminence in Lesotho. Figure 5 illustrates the principle at work in placings of this kind.[8]

During the internal expansion of the Koena lineage, there was a wide jurisdictional 'space' into which the Koena chiefs and their sons could grow, but clearly this process could not go on for ever: the time was reached, more quickly in some parts of the country than in others, when a jurisdictional plenum had been achieved. The whole hierarchy was now staffed by Koena chiefs who had been placed in wards by their fathers and paternal uncles. Moreover, the settlement and closure of the frontiers of Lesotho in the later nineteenth century meant that no new areas could be opened up by external expansion.[9] Wherever and whenever this point was reached, the problem of younger sons reasserted itself. New wards could not be created for them except at the expense of pre-existing chieftainships, and when these were already in Koena hands, new placings could only be at the expense of entrenched Koena rights. Either junior sons would be relegated to commoner status, or else they would be promoted at the expense of the senior heirs in junior collateral lineages. The placing system meant that this could be achieved without formally depriving the existing chief of his ward, though as we have seen after a few jurisdictions had been interposed between him and the chief who had formerly been his immediate superior, very

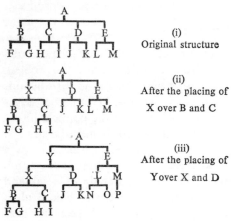

(i)
Original structure

(ii)
After the placing of
X over B and C

(iii)
After the placing of
Y over X and D

FIGURE 5   *The system of placing*

Note: By the time stage iii has been reached, while L and M have created minor chiefdoms under them, their collaterals F, G, H and I have been reduced to headman status, at best; their junior sons will certainly be commoners.

little was left of his previous status. In fact, it has been the regular practice of the more important chiefs in Lesotho to promote not only their heirs (who would succeed anyway and who therefore do not disturb the structure) but also their junior sons; the inevitable consequence of this was thus to advance the position of the senior descent line at the expense of the collateral lines, which were progressively demoted within the local hierarchy. This process served to hold in check the fissiparous tendencies that are inherent in a segmentary system, once a certain critical genealogical distance has opened between the segments; but just because of this, it is a tendency that contradicts the ideal retrospective and non-repetitive principle defining this model of chieftainship seniority. The placing of junior sons, accompanied by the depression of collateral successors, thus hints at a very different way of reckoning seniority, based on propinquity to the reigning house *of the day*; instead of 'looking backwards', a man can look 'round about', and calculate his position in terms of the criterion that is here given the name of 'circumspective'. If this principle is, in its turn, expressed in ideal form, it gives rise to a pattern of ranking of the kind illustrated in figure 6, where the retrospective reference to Moshoeshoe I and the cardinal lines set up once and for all by him has given way to a circumspective reference to the Paramount Chief of the day. Such a system is clearly repetitive at every level, and would, if fully realised, result in the

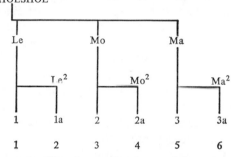

FIGURE 6 *The circumspective model*

'shunting off' into virtual oblivion of all chiefs of other cardinal lines supernumerary to the wards available.

Now, although the circumspective principle can be seen at work at many levels of the hierarchy, it has never operated at the level of the cardinal lines in such a way as to threaten the position of the houses of Molapo, Masopha and Majara. It has never been really conceivable that a Paramount Chief could place one of his sons over one of the cardinal houses. The successor to the Molapo chieftainship can thus plausibly describe himself as the 'second chief' in Lesotho. However, though it has been politically impossible for the Paramountcy to act invasively at the expense of the cardinal chiefdoms, it has secured a pre-eminent position for itself in other ways. As we have seen, the house of Letsie holds twelve of the twenty-two Principal Wards, and much the greater part of the entire land area of Lesotho. Each succeeding Paramount, in fact, has set up new Principal Chiefdoms, creating them out of the vast areas (relative to the country as a whole) passed down from Letsie. The beneficiaries of these major placings have been the sons and brothers of the Paramount Chief, so that their appointment has always stressed the circumspective principle of seniority *within* Letsie's house. Moreover, as close agnates of the Paramount, brothers and half-brothers of the reigning chief laid claim to a *national* position which could be legitimated only on circumspective grounds. For example, the present King's half-brother, placed as Principal Chief of Likhoele, plausibly regarded himself, and was plausibly regarded by many others, as the 'second chief' of Lesotho, though in terms of the cardinal structure he was no more than a relatively junior chief within the senior house.[10] An earlier but still modern example of the ambiguity surrounding the relative status of 'cardinal chiefs' and 'junior Royals' occurs in the recommendations concerning the salaries of chiefs as these are stated in the 1944 *Basutoland National Treasury Explanatory Memorandum* issued by the Paramount Chieftainess Regent. In most cases, salaries were calculated in proportion to the number of tax-payers within a Principal ward; but special exceptions were made for two Principal Chiefs. One of these was Bereng, the junior brother of the deceased Paramount Chief Seeiso and the second son of Griffith; the memorandum describes Bereng as 'the senior chief in Basutoland after the Paramount Chief' and accorded him the special allowance of £1,700 per annum. The other was Majara, the successor to the fourth cardinal line of Moshoeshoe's sons. He received a special salary of £300 per annum, on the grounds that the capitational sum would be too low for 'a Chief of his status in the house of Moshoe-shoe'. Here, both the circumspective and the retrospective principles can be seen at work—though it will be remarked that Bereng's salary as a Royal was put at a very much higher level than that of the cardinal successor, Majara.

The senior cardinal line after Letsie is represented by the house of Molapo. We have seen how the successor to this house can plausibly claim to be the 'second chief' in Lesotho, thus denying that status to the brother of the reigning Paramount; and, historically, the house of Molapo has always represented the strongest challenge to the circumspective claims of the first house. Molapo chiefs and spokes-men have always argued on the basis that the cardinal lines are more or less autonomous, the Paramount throne being no more than a symbol of Sotho nationhood and enjoying simply a primacy of honour outside those areas that fall within Letsie's domains. After the royal capital was established at Matsieng, a Molapo advocate is found referring to the Paramount Chief and his advisers and immediate followers as 'the Matsieng section', treating the Paramountcy as simply one, albeit the most senior, of the cardinal lines derived from Moshoeshoe's sons.[11] At the same time, however, a contradiction opens up in the position adopted by the Molapo chiefs. While they stress the autonomous rights of the cardinal houses, they resist any extension of this logic that might tend to support the claims made by subordinate authorities *within* the cardinal jurisdiction. Internally, the Molapo chiefs have promoted their own close agnates to the detriment of collateral chiefly lines, and have sought to display within their own ward the very prerogatives which they blame the Paramount Chief for attempting to exercise in Lesotho as a whole. In other words, they adopt a retrospectivist view in relation to the royal house, but a circumspectivist one within their own jurisdiction.

In maintaining its claim to a wider jurisdiction than the house of Molapo would concede to it,[12] the Paramountcy has been able to rely not only upon certain rights arguably supported by tradition but also upon the 'extrinsic' acts of the colonial power. The British authorities nearly always tended to support the Paramount Chiefs, no doubt for reasons of common political prudence; and the territory could be administered with less trouble if the Resident Commissioner had one centralised ruler to deal with at national level. One significant moment in the constitutional history of the relations between the colonial administration and the chieftainship was the promulgation of certain far-reaching and in their own way revolutionary statutes in 1938. Some further aspects of the 1938 Proclamations will be discussed in subsequent pages, particularly those that relate to the changes in the structure of the courts. Here, we will attend to the attempt made to cope with the confusion now apparent in the 'placing' system and to the new powers given to the Paramount Chief.

The contradictions that became apparent in the placing system once a jurisdictional plenum had been widely attained have already been examined. From the point of view of the colonial and indeed of some of the indigenous authorities, the chieftainship structure was in a hopeless confusion, with a proliferation of jurisdictions and a baffling multiplicity of wards. The object of the 1938 Proclamations was to re-write the law of chieftainship, putting chiefly office on a statutory basis and limiting the now essential 'recognition' of chiefs to those included on a gazetted list. The gazette itself, however, had to be drawn up by consultation with those chiefs, who were in fact the most senior ones, whom the colonial government regarded as best able to say who should be included and who should not. The consequence was that the gazette did not reflect the actual state of affairs immediately preceding its publication so much as that state of affairs which the chiefly advisers wished to see; from this point of view, the 1938 Proclamations were an accelerated and statutory extension of the placing system carried through by the administering authority. Some of the consequences have been well described by Patrick Duncan (1960) as follows:

[The 1938] Legislation need not have derogated in any way from established rights; the gazette list might have been drawn up with great care on the principle that all with *litokelo* (rights) would be included. . . . That has however not been done and from a glance at the various lists . . . it is clear that no consistent criterion has been followed of what is, and what is not, a chief or headman. . . . In Leribe possibly between a half and three-quarters of those who have in Sesuto law *litokelo* have been omitted from the gazette. . . . A list drawn up administratively has extinguished rights which in many cases are of great material value, which are highly esteemed for the status which they confer, and which in many cases have belonged to the families in question beyond the span of human memory (Judicial Commissioners' judgment in *Mathealira* v. *Tumo*, JC 135/51).

As this passage indicates, the decision on recognition was an administrative matter, and was not open to challenge in the judicial courts. (The profound disturbance which this restructuring of chieftainship had on Lesotho, and the dire consequences that followed, are analysed in G. I. Jones's outstanding report (1951) on the medicine murders that occurred in the 1940s and early 1950s.) At its worst, the 1938 legislation had the unanticipated and unintended effect of giving the major chiefs *carte blanche* to reconstruct the political system to their own liking.

However, the introduction of recognition and gazettement as a criterion of lawful office did not directly add to the power of the Paramount Chief over the nation generally. What did more positively support the position of the throne was the granting to the Paramountcy of the right to issue Rules and Orders with statutory effect, and from this grant a considerable volume of subsidiary legislation, much of it of major importance, has resulted. In the particular form that this power takes, it is of course a recent and extrinsically derived innovation; but it nevertheless seems permissible to regard it as a stage in the successful advance of the Paramountcy to a position of political pre-eminence of nationwide range and scope, since it can be seen as a case of the Paramount Chiefs conscripting the British authorities into supporting their claim to an ever wider and more effective control over the whole territory.

Such, then, are some of the general dimensions of the central, circumspective power of the Paramount Chief; like the placing system, they tend to depress the claims of subordinate and collateral lines, though like the placing system again they have not proved so

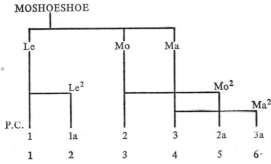

FIGURE 7   *The mixed system*

dominant as to offer any real threat to the basic integrity of the other cardinal houses. The political realities of the cardinal lineage structure and its effective legitimation in retrospective terms determine the limits of the circumspective principle, and of the claims and pretensions of the Paramountcy. Neither principle taken by itself furnishes an adequate account of the ranking of chieftainship seniority or gives a full explanation of the political structure in its relationship to agnatic descent. The effective seniority system, the empirical as opposed to either of the ideals, can best be described as 'mixed'. This gives rise to a partly retrospective, partly circumspective system, of which figure 7 offers a formal, diagrammatic representation.

The difficulties and ambiguities that exist for the purposes of calculating chieftainship seniority and jurisdiction are found also in the law governing succession to chiefly office. The present law is that stated in the 1959 edition of the so-called *Laws of Lerotholi*—

a self-styled 'declaration of Sotho law and custom' drawn up by a committee of Basotho members of the Legislative Council, but in spite of its inevitable deficiencies always a good starting-point for inquiry (for the history of the *Laws of Lerotholi* see Poulter 1972). Section 2 states that

> The succession to chieftainship shall be by right of birth; that is, the first born male of the first wife married; if the first wife has no male issue then the first born male child of the next wife in succession shall be the chief. . . . Provided that if a chief dies leaving no male issue, the chieftainship shall devolve upon the male following according to the succession of houses.

This statement of the law seems to make a clear assertion of primogeniture with reference to the order in which the wives (in a polygamous marriage) were married; and this is probably the law that is effective today. (For example, the last full Paramount Chief, Seeiso, had no male issue in his first house. The eldest child born to his second house is the present King, Moshoeshoe II. Seeiso also had a son Leshoboro in his third house who was born before the King, and is thus older than, although junior to, him.) But the statement in the *Laws of Lerotholi* has itself a history, and it would be wrong to suppose that the law of chieftainship succession is even now free from ambiguities. Patrick Duncan has informally but very reasonably written that 'the traditional law controlling succession might be described as "heredity modified by expediency". That is to say, normally succession would be by heredity, but if a chief were totally unsuitable, particularly in a crisis, he would be passed over in favour of a better man, preferably a member of his own family' (1960: 49). The history of the years following the death of Moshoeshoe in 1870 is in part the history of the growing ascendancy of the principle stated in the *Laws of Lerotholi*. This ascendancy was achieved across political conflicts, though it was argued in legal terms; and its eventual triumph should be seen more as the culmination of a historical process than as simply the full implementation and recognition of any certain and pre-existing law.[13]

The conflict began even before Moshoeshoe's death. The old King did not wish the succession to pass from his heir Letsie I to his grandson Lerotholi; the latter was the senior son of Letsie's second house, there being no male issue in the first. Moshoeshoe attempted to pass the succession through the *daughter* of the first house.[14] In the event, the plan failed and Lerotholi in due course succeeded his father as Paramount Chief. One of Lerotholi's first acts was to issue a declaration of law and custom, in which Law One stated the law of succession in terms very similar to those in the 1959 edition, quoted above. Duncan seems justified in commenting that 'it may . . . be assumed that Lerotholi's desire was that his new council ought to record the custom of descent through the male line' (1960: 44).

A particular point of interest in Lerotholi's succession concerns the composition of the group convoked to determine the matter. It is a universal principle in Lesotho that all matters of inheritance and succession are considered, at least in the first instance, by a council of the 'family' (*lelapa*). Normally, this family council is a group of somewhat indeterminate membership, in which however the brothers of the deceased usually play a lead. In general, the principle is that the closer agnates have the most weighty voice in the discussion.[15] Now, this has important implications where the Paramount Chief is concerned, since it could be, and indeed as we shall see has been, argued that his national position is of such general concern and importance that the 'family' and the 'close agnates' should not be defined in such a way as to give undue prominence to the personal agnatic family of the deceased ruler. To argue in this way is particularly consonant with a retrospectivist view, since it identifies the 'family' of the Paramount not by reference to his actual agnatic kin but by looking back to Moshoeshoe's own sons, to the cardinal lines, and considering these or their successors to carry the most weight in the council. On Letsie's death, the council consisted largely of Letsie's own sons, and it was on the advice of the Resident Commissioner that this group was expanded: instead of the decision lying with the 'Sons of Letsie', it was enlarged to include the 'Sons of Moshoeshoe', incorporating a wider range of agnates whose composition implied a recognition that the choice of the Paramount Chief lay not with the immediate 'family' of the deceased but with the larger descent group traced from the founder of the lineage.

Other problems were raised on the death of Letsie II in 1913, which illustrate some of the many difficulties that surround the question of identifying the heir, especially in a polygamous society. Letsie II left an infant son and no other male issue, and the child died while discussions were still proceeding. This left the way clear for Letsie's junior brother, Griffith, to claim the Paramountcy for himself. Griffith was, moreover, supported by the Sons of Moshoeshoe

CL—D

in demanding that he should succeed as Paramount Chief in his own right, to 'sit on the throne with both buttocks', rather than as regent for any successor who should eventually emerge. That such a successor might appear was a real possibility, since it was, and probably still is, a clear provision of Sotho law that a widow who enters into a leviratic union (called *kenelo*) with a brother or other close agnate of a dead man can raise up issue who are, in law, the children of the deceased. Griffith was determined that his succession to the throne should not be open to subsequent challenge by or on behalf of a posthumously conceived son born to a widow of Letsie.[16] His success in maintaining the position which he decided to adopt has been variously interpreted and has served to introduce further complications into the law of succession. It can be taken as an abrogation of the custom of *kenelo*; or it can be regarded as meaning simply that *kenelo* is of no effect in overturning a decision that was finally made at a point of time when no leviratic issue had yet been born.[17]

Griffith, in his turn, attempted to modify the law giving the succession to the first male child of the first wife married, when he attempted to divert the succession from his son Seeiso to his older son Bereng. In the service of this desire, he advanced arguments tending to show that there were defects in his own marriage to Seeiso's mother; and although he was, in the event, unsuccessful, the frustration of his original wish should probably be seen as a stage in the development of the law rather than as the simple victory of an already known rule over unlawful political ambition. Both on the occasion when Griffith sought to have Bereng proclaimed as his heir, and also when the decision was made for Seeiso after Griffith's death, a plenary meeting of the Sons of Moshoeshoe was called, and the matter was not left to the decision of the inner lineage of Griffith's own immediate agnates.

Seeiso died in 1940, leaving an infant son (now King Moshoeshoe II), and the issue of regency was raised. The same Bereng, Seeiso's junior but elder brother, claimed the regency, and maintained that the decision lay with the immediate members of the deceased chief's family. He failed in both demands. The decision was made by all the Sons of Moshoeshoe, and the regency passed to Seeiso's first wife, 'Mantsebo, who was, as it happens, without male issue and therefore not the mother of the infant heir. She reigned as Regent until the young prince took the throne in 1960.

The complexities of the customary law of marriage are such that there is often room for argument about the identity of the successor. In the present law, wives are ranked in the order of their marriage; but, although this principle has traditionally had an important place in Sotho law (which differs in this respect from the case of the Swazi Kings, Kuper 1947), the matter is not entirely settled. Ashton's view that 'nowadays, the first wife is always the senior wife, but formerly this was not always so' (1967: 193), is as good a way of avoiding the issue as any other. Some people argue that Koena wives are senior to non-Koena, despite the order in which they were married.[18] Further complications are introduced by the institution of secondary marriages; for instance, where a wife dies childless, her family may be asked to provide a sister of the dead woman as a substitute, and this *seantlo* wife, as she is called, may be taken into the house of the deceased and take precedence accordingly. Even where the original wife is still alive, a new wife may be married for her house, and again her seniority would be reckoned by reference to the house into which she was introduced. It is sometimes argued that the real determinant of seniority, especially among the first three wives, is the *completion* of bridewealth (*bohali*) payments, so that a woman married second might rank as the senior wife if the whole *bohali* debt in her respect had been discharged first. Marriage to the grave and woman-marriage are other (now obsolete) forms of secondary marriage; and we have already briefly considered the levirate (*kenelo*). Still further room for argument appears in the not uncommon practice for the issue of one house to be adopted into another; this tends to happen when a senior house is childless, and a son is taken from a junior house and promoted, usually as heir and successor, to the more senior one. These are some of the ways in which there is generous scope for legal argument, as well as debate on the facts, in the determination of succession to chieftainship. Within certain limits, any one of a variety of candidates can be chosen by the 'family' and the choice subsequently legitimated in terms of the law. Moreover, these issues logically preceded the more general issue of whether the emergent successor, once identified, is to take his seniority within the hierarchy from the application of the retro-spective or else of the circumspective principle in the determination of rank. We must now return to this fundamental issue and consider it in a rather wider context.

As we have seen, the two principles of seniority are not fully compatible, yet they enjoy a degree of *de facto* coincidence that permits them to coexist over wide areas of the political structure without overt tension. Difficulties arise when the two systems come into conflict at a point where important interests are threatened. At such a point, a decision between the two systems, or a compromise capable of interpretation in terms of either, must be found. Many Basotho adopt (at least in theory) the circumspective principle, and many the retrospective; but the actual ranking suggested in practice will be found to correspond to neither. When the inconsistency is pointed out, the discrepancies between the theory and the actual ranking produced will be accounted for (perfectly correctly at one level of analysis) in terms of historical or other accidents. The empirical situation will generally be described in a similar way by all local observers, but will be interpreted according to one view of seniority or another, the choice being only occasionally determined by whether the speaker will tend to gain from the theory he adopts. But from whichever standpoint of the two the empirical situation is initially approached, the 'accidents' themselves can be viewed as generating the alternative principle, and that is the analytical method that has been pursued here. Each principle exists as a descriptive item in the field. The tension between them, and their coexistence, and the duality of the system of seniority determination are, however, analytical concepts and do not exist 'on the ground'.

The retrospective principle makes possible a structural and administrative continuity, in terms of both the political and the kinship system, in that it envisages a continuing hierarchy, persisting territorially and in time, and conforming to patrilineal descent groups, which permits an exact and unambiguous reading-off of any individual chief's position, once his relationship to Moshoeshoe I is known. Such continuity could not be achieved in a system which gave each succeeding Paramount Chief the power to 'start afresh', nor could such a system be accommodated to the kinship institutions and the general law of succession, both of which are effective throughout Sotho society. The retrospective system reaches its *terminus ad quem* only when lineage segmentation has produced (by lower-level repetition at generation intervals) so many candidates for position that further jurisdictional subdivision ceases to be feasible. The lower levels of the hierarchy are then easily 'shunted off' into commoner status by applying the principle of primogeniture to exclude younger sons—i.e. at this level, the system becomes 'purely' retrospective and non-repetitive. Younger sons of chiefs are frequently in this position. From this point of view, the placing system is an acceleration of the 'shunting off' process, applied circumspectively by the Paramount Chief.[19]

The retrospective principle, since it takes Moshoeshoe as its point of reference and ranks seniority in terms of cardinal lines, indicates, and indeed by its logic implies, the primacy and seniority of the Paramountcy, yet at the same time it maintains the localism of chiefly government, which is an inescapable necessity of administration in a territory of nearly 12,000 square miles and more than three-quarters of a million resident inhabitants, where communication is rendered slow and difficult by the mountainous and in places almost inaccessible terrain.

The conceptual unity of the chieftainship in Sotho consciousness is a fact of ethnography. It can be incorporated into this analysis in terms of both principles of seniority, each of which represents the one *borena* (chieftainship) as existing on different levels and in different degrees; but whereas retrospectively considered the source of this 'diffraction' lies in Moshoeshoe I, or rather in his institution of the cardinal lines, circumspectively considered it lies in the Paramount Chief as Moshoeshoe's successor. Yet the process of lineage segmentation, central to the retrospective system, threatens this unity by producing (as it has in fact produced) a tendency to separatism as the descent groups move away from each other. The circumspective principle holds this tendency in check by relating seniority to the Paramount Chief in person and authorising him to override separatist forces, while at the same time a retrospective counter-reaction prevents this process from converting the hereditary chieftainship into an *ad hoc* bureaucracy. In this way as in others that have been noticed, the retrospective system tends to represent lineage *authority*, the circumspective to represent chiefly *power*.[20]

The circumspective focusing of attention upon the living Paramount Chief also centralises administrative control in him; the balance between this centralisation on the one hand and the localism of chiefly government on the other makes possible a system which respects kinship and succession without permitting segmentary anarchy, and maintains the political unity of the nation in a manner obedient to, and moulded by, the facts of Lesotho's topography.

The circumspective principle runs into the ground when the assessment of seniority by reference to the Paramount threatens the essential interests of the other cardinal lines, especially where new placings are involved. It is at this point that the interplay between the two principles brings about the situation represented in figure 7. This 'mixed' system can perhaps serve as a more accurate model of Koena chieftainship than either of its two analytically pure rival constituents; the analytical separating out of the constituent models illustrates the political functioning of the mixed system to advantage, by clarifying the separate features of each of the conceptual schemes that underpin it. But whereas each of the two constituent principles is susceptible to legal formulation, their resultant, the 'mixed' system, has not been so formulated or defined. It only attains visibility at points of tension between the retrospective and circumspective criteria—in other words, at points of choice and decision. The logical tension (or balance) between the two principles of seniority determination is the context in which certain political oppositions are expressed, and although the oppositions can naturally only be resolved politically, that resolution can then be legalized in terms of either the one principle or the other. The two find their point of coincidence in Moshoeshoe, whose ambivalent position—founder of the 'once-and-for-all' fraternal lineages; or else pattern for subsequent chiefs to *repeat*—is the model of the other ambivalences and ambiguities detected in the political system, and enables any empirical decision to be explained and justified by reference to him.[21]

3   The law of private succession and inheritance

The title of this chapter should not be taken to imply that there is a neat distinction, or in many respects any distinction at all, between 'private' and 'public' law in Lesotho. But it is convenient to use this term as a purely indicative label for those aspects of succession that are not covered in the chapters dealing with chiefly succession and seniority, and with administrative titles to land. We have seen that some uncertainty exists whether issues of chiefly succession should be determined in the same way as issues of succession within a subject lineage, or as issues of inheritance of discrete items of property. The retrospective principle tends to stress the interests of the wider lineage in chieftainship affairs and to distinguish chiefly succession from 'private' matters, where the immediate agnatic family decides. The tendency has been to move towards a more 'public' set of procedures in issues of chieftainship, especially in the case of the Paramountcy; but this should be seen as part of a continuing process, more apparent at certain levels of hierarchy than at others, and should not be interpreted as implying any radical theoretical discontinuity between 'public' and 'private' rights. Nevertheless, there undoubtedly exist certain points where a fairly sharp distinction can be drawn. For example, the so-called chieftain-ship lands, *masimo a lira*,[1] do not belong to the personal patrimony of the chief; and it is involved in the placing system that the ad-ministrative rights of chiefs—since they can be curtailed and ulti-mately abrogated when a superior is 'placed'—are distinct from the chief's own possessions and personal rights. The whole of customary land law is posited, as we shall see, on a denial of personal owner-ship in respect of all titles to land.

This has implications for the rights of subjects, too, since the nature of their rights to land is crucially different from their rights to cattle, to personal and household goods, and to the other items that fall within the concept of *lefa* (inheritance). The paradigm case of

45

such property, for the Basotho as for other southern Bantu peoples, is found in cattle, and much of what follows either refers directly to this form of wealth or can be transposed into its terms.

The present chapter, then, is principally concerned with *lefa*, and with those other incidents of inheritance and succession that are related to or derived from this category of right.

Much of the law of inheritance and succession could be expressed in terms of three well-known Sotho legal maxims:

(1) Houses do not eat each other up (i.e. invade each other's rights, destroy each other).

(2) Rights pass from the senior house to the junior.

(3) The heir and successor succeeds to the debts or liabilities too.

To these, could be added a fourth principle: a man does not die (*monna ha a shoele*)—that is, there is always a successor.[2]

The customary law of succession could be described and analysed very largely in terms of these legal proverbs. The fact that they are not at all points fully consistent with one another only reinforces their importance and makes them the more appropriate, since it is at the points of collision, and within the interstices of their ambiguities, that the real essence of the law as a living institution in society is most faithfully expressed.

Commentators have encountered great difficulties in seeking to give a definitive account of the Sotho law of succession.[3] Some of these difficulties are real, but many of them are the product of the commentators themselves, who too often embark on an erroneous quest for substantive rules of universal applicability. As has been argued earlier, there are legalities indeed, but these take the form of principles that are at once *general* and *concrete*, whose application and specification in particular cases depend upon a very wide range of facts, for the most part peculiar to each individual situation. The search for a fully deductive system is misplaced; it will be argued in the final chapter that this is always and especially true in a society where roles themselves are not fully 'specified', and where as a consequence it is never quite possible to isolate matters of 'relevancy' in such a way as to provide an armoury of rules enabling decisions to be arrived at as it were 'in advance' of the facts. Furthermore, the application of a *general* rule to a particular case does not have the effect of specifying or narrowing the law in other 'like' cases, since 'likeness' is a function of what it is that is regarded as importing a *relevant* comparability, and this criterion is not available in Sotho law below a fairly high level of generality. Indeed, it is often exactly where (for example) the heir's rights and the widow's claims collide that the law of succession and inheritance proves itself to be the servant of the living society that generates it.[4]

It would be little more than a venial exaggeration to say that the only really valid, customary and 'universal' rule contained in the provisions of the current *Laws of Lerotholi* is found in section 14 (4), where it is laid down that any dispute over inheritance and succession must go before the family council of the deceased. This is a traditional rule, and it is in the attempt to get back behind this crucial and central procedural requirement and to specify the substantive rules to be applied that most of the recent explorations in this field have been mistaken. It would be going much too far, of course, to claim that there are no substantive 'rules' of customary law at all; an attempt will be made below to ascertain and describe them; but they are, like nearly all customary 'rules', not really 'rules' at all, but norms, at once general and concrete, expressing principles that are held to activate and inspire the decisions in particular cases. In many respects, the current *Laws of Lerotholi* are a very respectable attempt to render these visible and articulate.

Obviously, the concept of 'ownership' is fundamental in any discussion about property rights. However, a lawyer finds it very difficult to match the categories in which common-law or civilian systems handle this concept to the categories employed by the Basotho. In many respects it is impossible to equate 'ownership' to any Sotho category. For example, there is no exact Sotho translation of the word 'own' especially in relation to the difference between 'own' and 'possess'. 'To have' is *ho ba le*, formed from the copulative verb ('to be') with the addition of the conjunctive *le* (with). 'I have a cow' is *ke na le khomo*, but there is no definite implication of 'ownership'. The word *rua* means 'own' or 'possess', but with the connotation of being rich, owning much (cf. English 'landowner'). The nearest word for 'owner' is *mong* (plural *beng*),[5] but this too has the implication of mastery or lordship rather than simple ownership. The word *mong* is also used in senses where the word 'owner' would not be used in English, e.g. in describing a husband and wife as 'owners' of a marriage, or of a case (*nyeoe*). The usual way of asserting a right to something is simply to say, *ke ea ka*, 'it is mine' (literally, 'it is of me'). But this does not necessarily carry any implication of ownership;

thus, the Basotho courts will say that a certain land 'is so-and-so's', although arable land is not capable of ownership. The 'belonging to' asserted here is posited *against* some other or alternative claimant.

Nothing of this means, of course, that the Basotho have a permissive attitude to theft, or that they are in the smallest degree uncertain of when some item or right does *not* belong to an interloper who claims it. In quarrels over property of every kind, the Basotho are a supremely litigious society, with an extremely highly wrought consciousness of rights and a lively resentment of any invasion of them.[6] But within what in a particular matter is taken to be the primary affinal and/or agnatic group, the concept of ownership is not used to discriminate between the rights of different group members. In an unreported case where a widow and an heir survived and it was a question of liability for *bohali* (bridewealth) in respect of a younger son, I was told 'The widow has the cattle, but they belong to the heir.'

Commentators, more particularly lawyers, have exercised themselves fruitlessly in the search for a clear explication of just such statements. Of course, there is an important sense in which the property of a minimal agnatic lineage is a common asset of the group; but this does not so much dissolve as pose the problem, since bitter disputes occur *within* such groups over the distribution and allocation of divisible items. Moreover, the widow is not an agnate of the deceased, his brothers or his sons, and her position in relation to the houses (huts), cattle or other wealth of her late husband is contingent and non-inheritable, yet it is above all in relation to her that the greatest complexities have arisen in determining the differential character of the rights of widows and heirs. From time to time the courts have tried to apply concepts of 'usufruct' and 'estate', but with inevitably limited success.[7]

The most satisfactory solution, if a solution in such terms is to be sought at all, is to regard the agnatic lineage, as a corporation, as the bearer of rights *in rem* over property and to treat all other individuals or sub-groups as titulars of rights *in personam* only.[8] The corporate lineage, of course, is of variable depth and range, and is moreover internally stratified, with some of its members bearing a greater authority than others. This variability of span and the internal differentiation of the lineage are reflected in the composition of the 'family council', the most visible expression of the corporate group, which comes together only on the occasion of death or of other major crises. Some consideration must accordingly be given to this council and its composition.

The council of the *lelapa* or 'family' consists essentially of the brothers (*bana babo*) of the deceased. Its exact composition, however, depends on the interplay of several other factors, such as the status of the 'family' involved and the importance of the matter of succession and inheritance to be debated, the social and geographical proximity of the various individuals who fall within the categories of persons who may attend the meetings, the history of individual and group relationships within the wider lineage, and even the personal predilections and preferences of influential members of the inner agnatic group.

The usual reference is to the 'paternal uncles' of the heir. The most important decisions obviously have to be made when the head of a senior segment dies, and since by definition all his brothers are in that event junior to him, each of the paternal uncles is often called *rangoane* of the heir, *rangoane* being the junior brother of ego's father. But an elder brother is entitled *a fortiori* (*ntate moholo*, the same term being applied to a paternal or maternal grandfather). Brothers include parallel cousins (in this context, patrilateral parallel cousins), and the lineage depth in terms of which these are defined depends on some or all of the factors that have been mentioned. We have seen in Chapter 2 that in the case of the Paramountcy, it has now been more or less settled that this definition is co-terminous with the national character of the office. The succession to a lesser chieftainship is an intermediate case, being less extensive in its implications than matters of succession to the higher chieftainships but much more 'important' than succession within 'private' or commoner lineages. In such cases, there is occasion for dispute over what is to determine seniority; whether this is to be 'circumspectively' defined, giving special weight to the immediate agnates of the deceased, or 'retrospectively', when the heads of collateral segments will rank higher than the junior members of the deceased's family; in fact, the outcome will usually be 'mixed', but the proportions of each component are a matter which cannot be deductively or predictively determined. Seniority is important, since the decision depends not simply on counting heads, but more centrally on the views of the senior members of the assembly. Age itself is a relevant factor here, too, length of years constituting one element in seniority.

Balanced with these considerations are practical matters such as geographical proximity or the existence of some special constraint such as illness, old age or poverty that might make it difficult for a person otherwise wanted and welcome to manage to attend; in such a case, however, if a suitable representative could be found, he (if also a member of the deceased's lineage) would often come in his principal's place. Where much property is involved, it is important that all transactions, allocations and decisions should be witnessed by as large a proportion of the agnatic group as possible. Where there is little inheritable wealth, or few dependants, or only light obligations, publicity is less essential. Indeed, it is particularly where much is at issue that the more distant agnates (in either a geographical or genealogical sense) are themselves most concerned to have a voice in the decisions that are made.

Again, an important factor in determining the catchment is the character of the relationship between the lineage segments, which again depends at least in part upon their physical and social proximity. Where brothers have stayed together for generations all who live in the cluster of associated homesteads will be members of the council. Where one brother has moved away from the others, his presence or absence will depend on the degree of his proximity, the seriousness of his disagreements with his agnates, and the extent to which his interest in the matter is seen to be that of a potential contributor or rather that of a forisfamiliated son who is only anxious to take what he can before severing his links entirely. (Inheritances, of course, are potential occasions for disputes between agnates as much as they are matters for joint decision and co-operation.) By contrast, where the major lineage is geographically dispersed and there is insufficient community of interest in property to bring its segments together, the composition of the family council will be organised more tightly around the immediate agnates.

These extra-structural factors weigh much more heavily where non-agnates are involved. The mother's brother (*malome*) of the deceased may have a voice in the family deliberations, provided that he has been a 'true *malome*' and not merely someone who simply falls into the category of mother's brother. To be a true *malome* is to take a personal interest in his nephew (*mochana*), helping him with his bridewealth and looking after his sisters. To be a *malome* in the relevant sense is as much an achieved as an ascribed role; and among the many *bo-malome* that a man may have, only a few will normally be brought within the intimacy of the family. Again, the *malome* will not as a rule have a voice in matters of public succession or participate in decisions that are internal to the agnatic family, or involving disputes between the agnates *inter se*. If the mother of the deceased is still alive, the *malome* will be concerned that she (his sister) is properly considered in the dispositions made after her son's death.

The *malome* of the heir also has a place in his capacity as an agnate of the deceased's widow or widows. Again, the widow's agnates are concerned more with those dispositions that effect their sister than with other matters, and (outside parallel cousin marriage) would not have a voice in decisions that were internal to the agnatic lineage of the deceased. But where a 'family council' met during the life of its senior member, the 'true *malome*' would have an important role, especially where decisions affecting his nieces and nephews were involved.

The adult sons of the deceased, and especially the heir, take a full part in the assembly, and in many matters of allocation and distribution the role of the principal heir (provided he is a major) is the most important of all. The wives of senior brothers and elder sons are also entitled to attend, though here as elsewhere the position and status of women must still be regarded as in a condition of change, so that it is difficult to propose any general rule determining the part that they are expected or permitted to play. Viduity itself confers rank and a degree of autonomy, so that (other things being equal) a woman's role will be the more influential if she is a widow, if among widows she is senior, and if her husband had enjoyed high rank among his own agnates. But here again non-structural factors enter, notably her seniority in years, the personal respect in which she is held, and the wealth or status of her own agnatic family.

The council of the *lelapa* thus consists of an indeterminate group of agnates and affines built round a core of 'brothers' of the deceased. It is not possible to specify a general rule defining its composition with greater particularity.

Another fundamental attitude characteristic of the Basotho, and linked again to the *generality* of customary norms, is the regular recourse to the requirement that disputants within the 'family' *must agree*. This stipulation replaces the specification of any substantive arrangements which they must *agree to*—and of course it is the latter which typically interest and concern the western lawyer in his approach to these problems; to him, it is precisely when disputants do not 'agree' that the law becomes manifest; whereas for the Basotho, such a breakdown within the family represents a situation not where the law is at last made clearly visible but rather one where it is most distorted and obscured. It is certainly the case that when this happens the disputants will fight their case with the greatest passion and tenacity, but it is an error to suppose that this is therefore the point where 'law' has emerged from 'private agreement'. The law, in the ideal case, defines certain parameters within which the anticipated agreement operates, and provides a battery of often inconsistent and sometimes directly opposed legal weapons, to furnish the various interests with a broad legitimation of their *general* position and claims. To that very significant extent, social relationships in matters of inheritance are 'law-governed' as they are, in principle, in other fields too. The Basotho, as has been noted, are not only litigious, they are lawyers, even legalists. They are all the more able to be so, by virtue of the very ambiguities of the law, which enable a variety of different claims to be advanced and different outcomes to be justified, on the basis of an overarching 'law' to which all assent.[9]

Both the *Laws of Lerotholi* and the traditional language of the Basotho in court and out of it make frequent use of expressions translated by such words as 'work with', 'use the estate with', etc. The word 'with' is, in fact, an accurate translation of the Sesotho *le*, and conveys just the indeterminacy which pervades the norms of customary law—e.g. in 13 (1), where the heir is obliged by custom to 'use the estate with his father's widow'.

Such 'laws' are, in fact, not to be seen as the stipulations of a code that is invoked *after* the breakdown of 'family' consultations—if they were that, they would be so unspecific as to be meaningless—but rather as the norms which are expected to be expressed *in* such private gatherings, and to determine the contours of the emergent settlement.

Traditionally, of course, if recourse were had to a court at all, it would be to the undifferentiated *lekhotla* (court) of the chief, where (as we shall see) what are now distinguished as judicial matters and administrative matters were not segregated.[10] The modern judicial court finds itself in a difficulty, since it conceives its function to be that of determining existing rights, whereas it is exactly because no rights *have been created* that the deceased's relatives have come to court at all: hence the anxiety of judges and magistrates to ascertain specific *rules* enabling them to *declare* rights abstractly and universalistically deducible from the law.[11] The view point of the chiefs' courts was quite different, and is aptly expressed in the words used by a Sotho court president in a case that occurred before these courts were overwhelmed by modern legislation:[12]

> I am proud that this case has reached me, as I am the distributor of estates. I am awarding these things in accordance with the law. If your father had died without giving this horse away, I would have divided it in two parts and each of you would have had his share.

Such disputes are, in fact, brought still to the chiefs' courts, either instead of or as a preliminary to the judicial courts, where matters can be conducted without the distractions of 'judiciality'. The chiefs' courts, in fact, act—or attempt to act—where family councils fail, or where there is no basis for consensus. New rights *flow from* the decisions[13] of such courts, much as they flow from a council of the 'family'. As I will argue in the concluding chapter, it is wrong to regard this situation as one where the (specific and determining) 'law' sets a framework for the operation of 'discretion' where legal rules do not operate. The decisions of the chiefs' courts flow from the law and are shaped by the general norms that characterise it.

A great deal of debate has gone on, both in the courts and outside them, as to the relative rights of widows and heirs in Sotho law. Much of the argument turns on the words used by George Moshoeshoe, one of Moshoeshoe I's sons, in 1872 (*Report and Evidence of the Commission on Native Laws and Customs*, Cape Town 1873). George stated that 'a widow can inherit cattle belonging to her house if she has no male children at the death of her husband.' What is meant by the concept of 'inheritance' here? Some light is thrown on this by the case of Paramount Chief Seeiso's herds. While still alive, Seeiso divided the bulk of his cattle between his first three houses; it will be recalled that he had no male heir in his first house, and that the present King was born the eldest son in the second house. When Seeiso died in 1940, 'Mantsebo, the senior widow and for the next twenty years the Paramount Chieftainess Regent, retained the cattle that had been allocated to her. When Moshoeshoe II acceded to the throne in his own right in 1960, he was unable to withdraw the cattle from the Chieftainess, but on her death in 1964 they passed to him as his father's principal heir.

Now, although 'Mantsebo had no sons, she had a daughter. As it happens, this daughter was already married, and moreover to a chief, and so was provided for; but had she been (somewhat improbably) left single, it might be thought to follow from George Moshoeshoe's statement ('a widow can inherit') that 'Mantsebo could have given or bequeathed the cattle to her. This interpretation would appear to be supported by the failure of the young Paramount Chief in his attempt to claim them for himself, and the court's decision that 'Mantsebo could retain them. But this would be to misread the law, and to mistake the Sotho concept of 'inheritance' for a right of 'ownership' in the Western sense. When a widow is said to 'inherit', this does not mean that she can alienate the property of the agnatic lineage. The significance of 'inheritance' is not what it might seem. Thus if, for example, it is assumed that a widow is left with no issue in her house, then George's opinion that she can 'inherit any cattle belonging to her house' appears either illogical or superfluous, since 'her house' consists simply of herself, and if they 'belong' to that house, she does not need to 'inherit' them. This goes to show the caution with which formulations like this need to be approached, and suggests a warning against the attribution of rights *in rem* to individuals—especially to women, and more especially to widows in polygamous families. 'Belonging' as used here refers to the allocation (*kabo*) of cattle to a house by the husband or other entitled person. At the time of the allocation, it is not normally known what issue will come to that house. Once the allocation has been made, the husband is obliged to 'use' that allocated estate 'for' the house in question, and this obligation survives him and passes to his heirs. The widow is thus a main beneficiary of the allocation and is protected in her enjoyment of the style of life made possible by it for the rest of her life. It is in this sense that she 'inherits' the property 'belonging to her house'.[14]

This account, though based on a continuing argument, represents the writer's own analysis of the position, and to a considerable extent departs from the indigenous conceptualisations both of the Basotho and of the Roman-Dutch courts. Basotho, and the Basotho courts, talk in terms of heirship, and frequently disagree both with each other and among themselves. At times, these disagreements concern the status of women, some adhering to the more restrictive features of the older law and regarding the *de facto* changes as foreign to Sesotho custom, others affirming that though there have been changes, these are either less radical than is claimed (since the old law was not in fact as restrictive as the others assert), or that such modifications are legitimate *changes in* custom, not abrogations *of* it. But, for much of the time, the disagreements are largely terminological and neither represent nor lead to any substantive difference in outcome. In one case, a Sotho court stated that 'under the customs of the Basotho the widow cannot become an heir' (Bb); in another, it stated that the estate of the deceased was 'still in the hands of the widow' (Cr), and in a third, that the widow, not the son, was the heir (Ae). Apparent contradictions of this kind could be multiplied. But they do not represent substantive disagreements at all. Whether the widow or the son is said to 'inherit' depends upon whose rights appear to be under invasion. In the first case referred to immediately above, the purpose of the judgment was to make sure that the widow did not alienate her late husband's estate in her house without consulting his agnates, so that it could be determined from which part of the estate—i.e. from which of the deceased's houses— the debt claimed was due. In the second case, a creditor of the late father sued for the return of some goats and their progeny, which had been lent to the deceased. The son appeared to think that the creditor was suing for the estate itself, as though disputing the inheritance. He claimed to be no more than his mother's guardian, her *molisa* (herdsman), since it was his mother who held the goats. The court pointed out that it was precisely as guardian that he was liable; the claimant had properly sued him as his father's successor. The goal of all these decisions is the same; to secure proper support for the widow[15] and at the same time to protect the property of the house, for the benefit of the son, successor and heir. During the joint lives of widow and son, that person can be said to have the right to 'eat the estate' whose position in the particular case appears to need protection or support. Equally, it may be necessary to deny the name of heir (*mojalefa*) to a person who is using his or her rights to the property in a way that causes detriment to the other.[16]

In polygamous households, the household head normally distributes part of his property—cattle being usually the main item, but other livestock figure too, as do articles of clothing and domestic furniture and blankets—between his various 'houses'.[17] Such property will eventually pass to the heir in each house. Distributions of this kind are called 'allocations'. However, not all the estate is normally allocated in this way. That part which is left unallocated at death passes to the 'principal' heir, *viz.*, the eldest son in the senior house with male issue. This unallocated estate is not earmarked to the widow of the principal heir's house but falls directly to him, provided he is of age (i.e. in traditional law, married). A problem that arises concerns what is to happen when the deceased had only one house. Is all the property to be regarded as allocated to that house? Or is it all unallocated property, which passes directly to the heir? An immense amount of judicial and juristic energy has been brought to bear on this issue. It is argued that if all the property is held to be allocated, the heir to a monogamous marriage is worse off than the heir to polygamy, since all the estate is earmarked to the widow. Against this, it is argued that if all such property is regarded as unallocated, the widow's position is very weak since she is left with nothing.[18] It will be apparent that in terms of the present discussion, both these arguments, and others couched in similar form, must be treated with some scepticism, since they are based on questionable assumptions as to what the debate should be about, and turn largely on the desire to locate the holder or holders of rights *in rem* to the estate. If the terms of the discussion are transposed in such a way as to be directed to the protection of the rights (*litokelo*) of the various persons involved (the widow and the issue, among whom primarily the heir) then much of the debate becomes irrelevant. The superior Roman-Dutch courts are reluctant to see the issue in this way, since the manner in which modern courts handle interpersonal issues is, so far as possible, to attribute predetermined and if possible 'real' or at least specific rights to the parties. The Basotho courts have kept close to the relevant concerns, declaring that it was a case for the family council, or (where matters have passed beyond that point) finding for the son but upholding the right of the widow to be supported by him from the estate (Ct).

It is not inevitable that the husband should make an allocation during his lifetime, but if he does so, he must stand by it and use the allocated parts 'for' the houses to which they 'belong'. But he must not allocate it in such a way as to deprive the principal heir of more than half the estate. This offers the heir some protection in his vulnerable position as universal successor, discussed below. Where there is no male issue, the property still attaches to the house until the widow's death, when it falls to the principal heir. Where there is male issue, the property of course remains with him after the widow's death.

If the estate has not been allocated at all, the unallocated entire estate falls to the principal heir; but as the *Laws of Lerotholi* section 13 makes clear, this does not acquit the heir of his obligations towards the other houses; rather, it places on him (subject as always in this area to the family decision) the duty which his father has left behind when he died. The principal heir for many purposes steps into his father's shoes—he is, in fact, a universal successor, and his position needs rather more careful and concrete scrutiny than the discussion so far has provided. But before specific cases are considered, some preliminary attention must be paid to the general nature of the heir's status as successor, a status which is expressed in the third maxim set out above, 'the heir and successor succeeds to the debts too.' In one case, the judge in the Basotho Court quoted this maxim and commented that it means that 'the heir . . . will make good his late father's debts, regardless of how much estate he has left behind' (Bs). The saying that 'a man does not die' reinforces this: there is always a successor. The obligations of succession apply not only to debts owed 'outside the family', but also, as has been said, to arrangements inside the family of the deceased. It is now necessary to see what may be involved in this. Real life situations are less unambiguous than the *Laws of Lerotholi* suggest, and it has of course been argued above that (quite apart from the exogenous character that marks certain aspects of these 'laws') the norms of customary law are not to be taken as rules governing every future eventuality. Thus, the *Laws of Lerotholi* as given do not disclose the possibility, and the consequences of the possibility, that the estate may have been allocated in such a way as to leave the junior houses well provided for, or that it may have left them with very little. What happens is that each case is looked at in the light of the customary norms of fairness between houses and obligations of support, and a decision made that flows from this consideration of the matter. Thus, David T.'s father died leaving a large number of beasts, which may be put at 250 as a round figure. Before his death, he allocated 50 to his second house and 25 to his third. He did not formally allocate any to his senior house. The 175 unallocated cattle stayed with the widow, and the heir lived with her. He looked after his mother and the cattle too. The two younger brothers also stayed in the same place and the cattle were all 'used together', though they took their cattle away with them when they left to establish their own households on marriage. If the heir leaves his mother's home, she should release some cattle to him—and, of course, they will all come to him on her death —especially where the heir had no cattle of his 'own', unallocated by his late father. Disputes would traditionally go before the 'family' and then on to the chief's court if no settlement could be reached. Normally, where a reasonable part of the estate has been allocated to junior houses by the deceased, the principal heir is not obliged to support these houses (e.g. by providing bridewealth for sons being married) out of the unallocated estate. If the heir himself discharges the duty of allocating a (wholly or largely) unallocated estate, he will take such debts into account in deciding how much support he can afford to let the junior houses have, as well as other factors such as the number of dependants to be supported in each house. And the heir is, of course, liable to look after his younger brothers in the junior houses. It is further his responsibility (as with all eldest sons) to support his own mother, no matter whether a part of the estate has been allocated or not.

These considerations raise the question of the relationship between houses, and recall the maxim quoted at the outset, that 'houses do not eat each other up'. We must now turn to the question of what kind of action or disposal actually constitutes such 'eating up'. Basically, what is forbidden is the use of the property of one house for the benefit of another, and the problem arises most frequently at a point where the houses have not yet emerged into full independence: where the heir of one or more of the houses is a minor, and the widow either dead or under the guardianship of the principal heir or of another agnate (usually brother) of the deceased. It is for example contrary to the maxim to take cattle from one house to provide *bohali* (bridewealth) for the son of another, and it is equally wrong to take *bohali* received in respect of a daughter of one house and put it into another. The position here is, however, complicated by the fact that if a man helps a junior with *bohali*, he can receive a portion of the *bohali* paid for that brother's sister: and a fruitful cause of dissension is whether such a transfer is the repayment of a debt, or the improper 'eating up' of a house. Where the estates are 'mixed up', for example where cattle are kraaled together, there is moreover no visible or physical separation of the houses. When quarrels supervene on a previously amicable arrangement, questions of house-property arise that are hard to sort out since the original facts have passed away or never been ascertained. It is largely for this reason that the houses of a deceased often physically separate out after the death, and most independent homesteads have their own kraals. Half-brothers, and brothers too, seek their own sites because of the need to identify their own property. But this physical separation will often not occur during the lifetime of the father, so that on his decease it becomes a question of recalling the details of his allocation. As with all such acts in the law, allocation requires publicity, and should not only be performed 'with' and in the presence of the heir and other agnates, but also reported to the chief. Nevertheless, questions of fact become matters of dispute when years have passed—especially when, as often enough, the original witnesses are absent or dead.

It is worth repeating that the maxim that houses do not eat each other up applies equally to the father during his life as to the heir after his death. The allocation to houses means, for instance, that *bohali* cattle must be taken either from the kraal of the groom's house or from that of the unallocated estate retained directly in the husband's hands. On his death, the maxim protects the *house-property* of the heir as well as that of junior houses. But it does not protect the *unallocated* estate, nor does it free the heir from his *personal* liability to discharge his father's debts, which he may have to do out of his own labour and wealth if the estate is not large enough to bear the charge.

The rule or maxim stressing the rights of houses is in tension with the principle that the successor succeeds to the debts or liabilities as well as to the assets of the estate. The aspect of the law which a disputant stresses will tend to reflect his view of his own interests. In one case, Albina claimed from 'Ma-Phiri two goats which, it was admitted, had been borrowed from him some years before. 'Ma-Phiri was her late husband's senior widow, and she replied that the goats had not been borrowed by her but by Moela, the son of one of her husband's junior houses; the debt therefore bound Moela's house, and 'Ma-Phiri was not involved. But the Paramount Chief's court differed: 'According to law, 'Ma-Phiri may not be forced to pay this debt with the property of her own house, but it is not for Albinas to say which house it is whose property must satisfy the debt. It is for 'Ma-Phiri to determine the family property that must settle the liability' (Bh). It is clear from this that although the heir (in this case, the heir's widow) is liable, this does not rule out his own recourse (in turn) to another source. The liability of the heir, while not permitting him to breach the rule of 'eating up', does not mean that he has no recourse to persons substantively liable.

Chieftainess 'Mamathe was involved in another dispute that raised this question (Bl). She is the widow of the late Gabashane, great-grandson of Moshoeshoe I's third son, Masopha (see figure 1), and at the time of the case was still Regent for her minor son; she thus represented the third of the 'cardinal' houses in the house of Moshoeshoe. The case was brought against her by one Zulu Rapopo, whose daughter was married to Liketso, heir to a junior house of Masopha I. The matter at issue was the bridewealth which Zulu claimed was owed to him by the chieftainess in her capacity as head of the house of Masopha generally. The Basotho court found in favour of the chieftainess, on the ground that 'it is not all the sons of Masopha for whose bridewealth the defendant is answerable'. However, the court also held that she had been properly sued, as regentess-head of the Masopha house, but she was not obliged to take the cattle out of her own kraal. The bridewealth still owing must come from the house to which Liketso belonged. Since this dispute involved collaterals linked only at considerable lineage depth, no question of any original unallocated estate from Masopha I could arise. The issue of succession on the one hand and house autonomy on the other was thus squarely posed. (The only complication that entered was that there was some evidence that 'Mamathe's late husband, Gabashane, had tendered some cattle to Zulu for Liketso's marriage. 'Mamathe denied this, and she may have been right; but at all events it would have been an entirely normal act for the senior chief of a cardinal house to undertake on a junior kinsman's behalf. Zulu's tactic was to represent this gift, if it was ever made, as proof of an obligation now falling upon the chieftainess as the successor-regent.)

Another case in which seniority in succession founded an argument that ran counter to the rule of house autonomy also involved bridewealth (Bu).

Here, Lerata argued that bridewealth in respect of his junior half-brother, Sekautu, was not due from himself but from Pakalitha, the heir of the senior branch of his grandfather Sepolo's lineage. It was, in this instance, in the interests of the disputant to stress the line of succession superior to his own, and to try to settle the liabilities away from his own house. He did not, of course, pursue the logic of this to the minimal lineage of which he was head; here, it was in his interest to recall the autonomy of houses.

Disputes such as these show how the norms of customary law,

being maintained at a high level of generality, can sometimes more and sometimes less plausibly come into apparent conflict. Parties stress one set of rules rather than another according to their perceptions of where their interests lie. Since the effect of a particular decision is not to supply a *ratio decidendi* narrowing the rule in its future application, the law returns to its generality when the case is over and furnishes subsequent litigants with as fully-stocked an armoury of juridical weapons as before. In some instances, of course, a particular litigant comes forward with a quite implausible case, and will often admit, out of court, that he had no serious expectation of success—he had brought the action for the chance of what he might win from it. But the plausible cases are much more common, and in these the Basotho courts will normally look to the question of who it is whose rights are being invaded—who it is who is under threat of being 'eaten up'—and decide accordingly. Words such as 'inheritance' (*lefa*) or 'heir' (*mojalefa*, literally, the eater of the in-

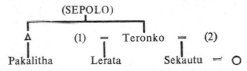

FIGURE 8   Mojake *v.* Litjamela

heritance) are not used with precision or consistency in the judgment that issues. The rules of law enable the decision reached by the court to be based on reasons, and legitimated by reference to a legal norm such as one or other of the maxims that we have been examining. But it does not follow that the decision is *constrained*, in the sense of being logically pre-determined, since the rules and maxims are not fully consistent when pursued to their conclusion and in the end one set of principles must be preferred to another. To be able to give a reason is not to postulate an efficient cause.[19] As we shall see in greater detail later, this does not mean that there is, on the one hand, a set of bounding rules organised in a deductive system, and, on the other hand, an area of free discretion which the rules simply circumscribe. To suppose that this is the case would be to imply 'decision-inevitability'[20] in regard to the rules and disorderly choice in their interstices; as subsequent chapters show, this is the view of Sotho law adopted by the official courts, and thence imported in varying degrees into the Basotho courts; but though 'political' considerations enter into the choice of norms, the implied dichotomy of 'law' on the one side and 'power' on the other fails to give a true picture of customary judicial practice. In the traditional system, all decision-making is—ideally, at least—informed by law. It is never enough to say, 'I will it so'; the judge must declare, 'I will it so, because . . . '.[21]

4 Land tenure

The fundamental principle of both the administration and the tenure of land in Lesotho is that 'the land belongs to the nation' (*mobu ke oa sechaba*). Of course, like all very general principles, this statement of the law would have no consequences if specific means did not exist for its concrete implementation. In Lesotho, the chieftainship is the institutional mechanism whereby the 'national' ownership of the land is given practical expression. The current Roman-Dutch conceptualisation is that the land belongs to the nation and is held 'in trust' by the Paramount Chief. The Paramount Chief is then thought of as delegating this trust to the higher chieftainship, who in turn delegate to their sub-chiefs and headmen (An). It will be clear from what was said in Chapter 2 that this is an excessively 'circumspectivist' view of the Paramountcy, since by any account the chieftainship has a more collegial character than this notion of royal delegation allows. It is more helpful to start from Sheddick's distinction between 'administrative' and 'usufructuary' titles (1954: 1–12). In these terms, the chieftainship has an administrative title to the whole land of Lesotho; this title carries with it the right to allocate land to persons or categories of person for use or cultivation in specified respects. The hierarchy of chiefly jurisdiction, outlined in Chapter 2, allots to every chief the specific responsibility for land allocation within the territorial area of his ward.[1] Strictly speaking, the proper land-issuing authority is the chief or headman with immediate jurisdiction over the area of land in question;[2] a superior chief cannot allocate land within the ward of his subordinates, though he can decide appeals arising from the decisions of lower chiefs and he can request, and in some cases require, a subordinate to allocate land in a particular way. In Sheddick's terminology, the beneficiary of a chiefly allocation—the actual landholder—holds a usufructuary title,[3] entitling him to use the land within the limits specified in the terms of the grant. Whenever a usufructuary title fails (through

63

death, removal, forfeiture or otherwise) the right reverts to the chieftainship for reallocation. But land which has fallen back to the chief in this way does not 'belong' to the chief; that is to say, it is not the case that the chief combines an administrative and usufructuary title in respect of all the land in his ward that is from time to time unallocated, nor that he is in any sense an 'owner' of such land (even if this ownership were understood subject to the rights of his superiors). It is still the case that 'the land belongs to the nation', and although a chief can indeed allocate land to himself, it is only in respect of such land that he can claim a usufructuary title. In other words, administrative and usufructuary titles are held distinct, even where no present usufructuary exists, or where they are both held by the same person.[4]

The national character of the soil and its resources is most clearly seen in what is called, in Sesotho, *leboella* (pl. *maboella*). The root meaning of the word is that of 'returning again', so that *maboella* are 'provisions kept for another occasion' (Paroz 1961: 42). So far as land resources are concerned, *maboella* and *liremo* include reed beds, trees and woods not allocated to particular households, and other similar sources of supply; but the term is most often applied to pasture-land, and more particularly to the mountain grazing grounds where cattle are driven for summer grazing and which are withdrawn from arable use. Grazing in these areas is permitted only at certain times of year, as laid down by the chief who controls them, but once the *leboella* is open, all those who fall within the permitted category in terms of chiefly allegiance can use them equally. *Leboella* constitutes a second and parallel resource, additional to that of arable lands, and it is one that is very highly valued (see Wallman 1969: 115). It differs from arable land not only in the sense that it is exclusively for pasturage but also in the sense that whereas (as we shall see) rights to lands are individuated and specific—a land-holder has the use of this or that identified field—grazing rights are essentially diffuse: all of a given category of person can use any of a large area of pasture, from the time the *leboella* is open until the onset of winter and the long trek home. The chief who has the right to open the *leboella* is administering a national asset, not manipulating a personal prerogative, or even choosing between one man and another as he does in allocating arable land. When the Chief of 'Mamathe's showed favouritism in allowing some of his subjects to graze the *leboella* and not others, the Paramount Chief's Court found against him, stating in terms that 'the *maboella* belong to the nation' (Bk). (On appeal to the Judicial Commissioner, the Chief was successful, the Court taking the view that though the chief's favouritism was deplorable and he had acted abusively, it was an administrative matter that fell within his discretion, and the judicial court could not interfere. This conclusion is a characteristic effect of the polarisation of legal right and administrative discretion imported by the judicial courts into a customary law to which it is quite foreign.)

However, though the rules governing *maboella* may represent the most general and far-reaching sense of the doctrine that the land belongs to the nation, it is arable land that constitutes the central concern of this chapter—and indeed of the Basotho themselves. From the point of view of the people, land—arable land—is the crucial economic resource. The life of Lesotho centres on the land. Much the greater part of those who at any given time are living within the country's borders depend on arable fields for their subsistence. What they cannot produce themselves must be imported at greater cost from the Republic of South Africa, and few can easily afford to augment their food supplies by purchasing provisions. The very many who are absent from Lesotho as migrant labourers in South Africa rely on the lands their families hold, or hope to obtain, as their ultimate security when they return home. The fact that the land is poor and its productivity low only makes it more precious since there is so little spare productive capacity in the nation that those without land can easily become destitute. The discussion in this chapter will therefore concentrate on arable land, on the chief's administrative role in relation to it, and on the rights, duties and expectations of their subjects.

In principle, every adult Mosotho (which means, strictly speaking, every married male) has a right to an allocation of arable land to provide for his subsistence and that of his family and dependants, and it is for the chieftainship to arrange for him to have this. A. J. B. Hughes (1964) uses the term 'right of avail' to describe this basic, very general right to a share in the resources of the nation. The right is accompanied by certain matching obligations. The subject owes allegiance to the chief who makes him a grant of land, and is required to reside within that chief's ward, or at least to maintain his presence there, if he himself is absent, through his wife, children or other kin.[5]

The obverse face of the duty of allegiance to a chief is the subject's power to withdraw from this allegiance and attach himself to another chief. At one time, this was an effective sanction. A chief needs subjects if his chieftainship is to have any real meaning, and in the period when Lesotho was being opened up and settled, and new jurisdictions created by new placings, subjects were in a position to exercise a real choice. This is much less true today, since expansion has virtually halted, and land has become a scarce resource.[6] It is true that in modern times it has become more possible for a subject to escape from chieftainship altogether, by seeking commercial or industrial or other employment, either in Lesotho or outside, but as we have seen, land still represents an ultimate form of security even for those who have no present need for it. The general claim on land resources is stronger than ever, and the role of the chiefs, as mediators of rights to land, remains central.

The diffuse 'right of avail' is without content until it is specified by a particular allocation. It is not a specific right to one particular field; nor, in the case of a stranger, does it imply even a general duty on any particular chief. Even one who is born into a given ward has still only a diffuse claim on his own chief, though it is the latter's duty so to administer the land in his area that all claimants, so far as possible, receive a share in the available arable acreage. The current pressures on land resources puts considerable power in the hands of chiefs and renders land administration both contentious and delicate. A great deal of litigation is concerned with claims to land, involving disputes either between subjects and chiefs or between subjects among themselves. (Disputes between chiefs normally concern quarrels over administrative rather than usufructuary titles.)[7]

Sheddick considers that the unit of allocation is what he terms a 'production unit'; in the case we are considering, this consists of the *arable rights over* a cadastrally defined land parcel, rather than the land parcel itself (1954: 3f., 10f.). He draws the distinction on the plausible grounds that after the harvest the occupier is obliged to open his fields to common grazing by the local community. This right of stover (*qheme*) is not allocated to any individual household, except in so far as he shares it with all the others in the entitled community. (One consequence of this is that arable lands may not be fenced.) The distinction which Sheddick draws between different types of production unit (of which there are more than the two mentioned here) has certainly considerable analytic value; but it is possible to make too much of it in relation to arable and stover rights. To insist on it for our present purpose would be to imply an indigenous view that does not in fact exist. People see themselves as having been allocated a land, though this allocation is subject to certain conditions: e.g., it is specifically for cultivation and not for building on. Similarly, arable land is *subject to* the right of stover, but this is seen as a burden on the land rather than as a separate unit of title. For most purposes, then, it is easier and simpler to treat the unit of allocation as a field or land, a defined area of soil.[8]

In theory, every entitled Mosotho has a right to three lands; but in practice many have to make do with less, or with none at all.[9] The average number of fields per holding (of all holdings with fields) is estimated at 2·4. More holdings have two fields than three, except in the border lowlands where the two categories are about equal. Well over half of all holdings have fewer than the acknowledged norm, and 3·7 per cent have no land at all. Even taking into account the fact that some persons (widows, residual families with adult children living away, etc.) may not be entitled to the full complement, there still remains a substantial number of people who experience a felt land-hunger that is also normatively legitimised. The norm of three lands is steadfastly adhered to, though it represents more a moral than an actuarial expectation. It means that a man with fewer lands considers that he has a good case for seeking more, and that a man with four or more must show special grounds for being allowed to keep all of them. A man with three lands is (other things being equal) in the proper condition of a Mosotho and can expect to be left with them.

It will be convenient to open the discussion of land tenure and the legal rights and duties associated with it by giving a brief statement of the general principles underlying it before moving on to the more contentious and theoretically interesting issues. Section 7 of the *Laws of Lerotholi* sets out the provisions of the current law in general terms. These can be re-ordered and re-stated as follows:

(1) A land-holder must receive his land from his chief, or his chief and headman, if any is available. It is, generally, a matter for the local chief to make the decision himself, but a subject can complain to a higher chief if he feels that he has been unjustly dealt with. However, the superior is unlikely to do other than leave the matter in the local chief's hands, unless the applicant has the superior's

support: in which case, however, the superior would probably have made a 'request' in advance, if he could not or would not allocate lands to him from his own direct area.

(2) Once a subject has been allocated land, he has a usufructuary title to it for life, subject to certain conditions. (a) He may lose his land if he removes from the area (i.e. ward, including headman's caretaking) where the land is situated. However, removal (though as will be seen it includes death) does not include the case where the land-holder himself leaves to work elsewhere, for instance in the Republic or in Maseru, provided that he leaves a member or members of his family (for example his wife) to look after the land during his absence. Many people, especially those in urban employment and living with their wives elsewhere, leave brothers or cousins to maintain title, and chiefs do not necessarily regard such people as 're-movers'. The test is rather the two-fold one that (i) the holder should continue in his allegiance to the chief, tax-payment being the generally recognised index of this and (ii) continue to occupy the land, through others if not by himself. (b) He must cultivate the land or cause it to be cultivated. Land is too scarce to waste, and if it lies untended for two successive years, it can be taken away after inspection and allocated to another, even if the holder continues to reside. (c) If the holder has more than he needs for his subsistence and that of his dependants, the chief may take the surplus away and re-allocate it. It should be emphasised, however, that the usufructuary title is not simply conditional. In principle, the holder has a secure lifelong title, and it is only if certain events occur that he loses it. The conditions, in other words, are strictly *resolutive*.[10] Again, an aggrieved land-holder can complain to the superior chief.

(3) Death counts as removal, except that the widow(s) and other minor dependants of the deceased have a right to continue to use the lands, though not necessarily all of them. A widow's entitlement is to two lands. Minor sons should be confirmed on the lands when they attain their majority, provided they remain under the same chief and fulfil the other conditions. Major sons have a special claim to the family lands, though this is weaker than the claim of minors, and again this is subject to the conditions of tenure.

Underlying these norms, lies the principle which, though easily overinterpreted and open to misunderstanding, nevertheless essentially contains one major component of the law: *ts'imo hase lefa*, 'land is not an inheritance'. The subtler implications of this are discussed below, but the broad meaning is that after a 'removal' or a forfeiture, the land reverts to the chieftainship for re-allocation, and cannot, when it has so reverted, be claimed as of right as an inheritance by any person who may nevertheless be an heir (*mojalefa*) for other purposes.

Land allocation

The chief is required to allocate lands through special land-issuers (*baabi*), and not do so directly or by himself (By). This is essentially an evidential requirement, to satisfy the need for publicity in land transactions (Am), and was of obvious importance when literacy was rare. Traditionally, land-issuers were appointed at the discretion of the chief and could be dismissed by him, and they have always been open to pressures for this reason. There is no way of determining what they choose to remember, misremember or forget. This is one of the ways in which chiefs can manipulate land-allocation and render their subjects' tenure less well protected than the rules make it appear. One of the easiest ways to deprive a man of his land is to declare that it had never been allocated to him in the first place, and land-issuers can regularly be induced to follow the chief's wishes in this respect (Ci). A variant of this tactic is to assert that the land in question had been simply *lent* to the subject on a temporary basis.[11] The Basotho Courts are suspicious of the whole principle of land-loans partly because they are open to this kind of abuse, but in a situation of land-shortage, strong social and economic arguments can be advanced in favour of maximum use and cultivation at all times. Under the independence constitution, land-issuers are no longer supposed to be discretionary appointments. Elaborate provisions have been introduced in an attempt to have them elected, at various levels of hierarchy, by the people of the ward in which they are to operate, but at the time of writing the evidence is that the scheme has met with limited success. In many areas, chiefs can exert pressures that virtually assure the election of the men they favour; and factionalism can prevent the mechanism of election from working at all (Ashton 1967: xxx f.; but see Hamnett 1967a).

Land allocation, strictly speaking, is made to married men only, and this rule is still usually adhered to by the Basotho Courts, though there is now a tendency for minority and majority to be assessed more in terms of years than of marital status. However, the

norm of three lands assumes that a man has married one wife; and
there is thus a sense in which an allocation is made in respect of a
wife, even though not actually *to* her. The question is finely balanced.
In one case, both the chief and the Basotho court upheld a wife's
claim that her husband could not lend a land to another of his
houses, since the land in question had been allocated in respect of
her marriage. In another, a divorced wife who was still in charge of
the children of the marriage succeeded in her claim to retain the
lands of her house in one Basotho court but lost it on appeal
to another (Av). Again, a Basotho court stated that 'lands are
allocated to the husband and not the wife; it is the husband who will
allocate them among the houses' (Aj); another declared that 'lands
are the property of a man and his wife; that means that when one of
his wives has died, the lands shall be annexed to the remaining wife
or wives' (Bt).

Part of the difficulty here arises from the ambiguity in the word
'allocation' (*kabo*) itself. It can be used to refer to the allocation of
land by a chief to his subjects; but it can also refer to the, so to
speak, 'private' allocation made by a family head among his houses
and dependants—for example, the allocation of parts of the estate
which we have examined in the last chapter. Now, it is true that (as
we have seen, and as we shall see again presently) lands are not an
inheritance and do not form part of the *lefa* or estate; but it is nevertheless within the authority of the family head to 'allocate' them
among his houses or his sons and other kin—i.e., to declare who has
the right and duty to cultivate them.[12] It is impossible to say with
much confidence how far such 'internal' family arrangements carry
over into the 'public' domain. This is all the more true inasmuch as
the chieftainship itself is still conceptualised at least partly in paternal
terms, and indeed in some smaller villages the roles of headman and
household head are virtually fused, the 'political' and lineage
components being indistinguishable. But even where the domestic
and public domains are distinct and seen to be distinct, the private
allocation of lands to houses and kin is an act that is expected to
survive the death of the family head in at least some of its effects.

The ideal allocation of three lands refers to a man with one wife.
Some people say that one land is for tax, one is for the 'house', and
the third is for the children. (Since tax liability starts at twenty-one
years, this view supports the argument that a bachelor is now
entitled to at least one land.) For each additional wife, there is an

ideal of two further lands. Once again, this does not reflect the actual state of affairs, and many large households have fewer lands than the ideal suggests. Nevertheless, it is on the whole true that the larger households have more lands than the smaller ones, and this indicates that overall the chieftainship does attempt to match allocation to need (Morojele 1962: Part 3, p. 59). Moreover, a large homestead group (nowadays more often an extended family than a polygamous household) can achieve certain economies of scale that go some way to compensating for the less than ideal allocation of lands.[13]

Although a married man is formally entitled to a full allocation, he is unlikely (even leaving aside the general shortage of land) to receive it if he continues to live in his parental homestead after marriage. He will be much more likely to receive one or two lands, and to be given the full complement (if at all) only when he moves out to establish his own homestead. This incremental pattern of allocation is well adapted to meet the changing needs in the developmental cycle. At first, before children are born and when they are very young, fewer lands are needed. As the children grow, more lands are required, and at the same time the children can help with the household economy, especially as herdboys. Quite often, by the time the father dies, the elder sons have married and moved away, in which case the youngest son may stay at home to look after the widow and eventually to inherit the site. (Such a person is known as 'the mouse among the ruins'. But although this is a recognised practice, there is no rule of ultimogeniture and the youngest son cannot claim to inherit the homestead site or the huts.) Meanwhile, it is not a clearcut matter to whom the lands 'belong'. A father often will retain more lands than he needs or is entitled to, in respect of married or allegedly about-to-be-married sons. This is again an area of uncertainty, where the borderline between chiefly allocation to a subject and private allocation within the family is unclear.

A chief or headman will sometimes take into account the possession of a garden site, particularly a large one, in considering allocations of land. As we shall see, gardens and building sites are legally distinct from lands so far as the rules of tenure are concerned, and applicants for land will resist the introduction of this issue into the case. This can also account for the fact that some potentially productive gardens are under-used or neglected. People who maintain themselves from their garden prejudice their claim to lands, since they already have enough for their subsistence. Since sites, as will be seen, are tenurially much more secure than lands and not subject to forfeiture for non-user, they can safely be allowed to deteriorate, while their owners continue to cultivate their lands.

Chiefs will also take into account factors such as length of residence in the village, birth within the ward or caretaking, and the existence of kinship or affinal links with those already established. But it would be misleading to ignore one further and very important element. Although land allocation is, in law, a gratuitous act, many chiefs, headmen and land-issuers both expect and receive payment for granting or confirming an application or claim to land. It is extremely difficult to gain first-hand information on this topic, since not only the chief and the land-issuers, but the land-holder too, will rarely admit to such a transaction. It is always an event that took place in another village, or something that was told about a relative or friend. On the opposite side, the complaints of an aggrieved land-holder have to be treated with a certain caution since such a person has an interest in alleging malpractice as the reason for his failure to obtain or keep a land. Nevertheless, there is no doubt that land allocation is regularly open to this kind of corruption, and that the incidence of bribes or other inducements to chiefs is widespread. These inducements cover a wide spectrum, from simple bribery at one end of the scale to the proffering of respectful gifts or services at the other. In the latter case, there is no clear line between 'improper' inducement on the one hand and the simple expression of allegiance on the other. Moreover, the abolition or attenuation of the chiefs' courts and of tribute-labour has modified the criteria of what constitutes loyalty and allegiance, and opened the system to what in many cases is an abuse that works most powerfully against those in greatest need, since it is these who are least able to afford the price expected.

We have already noted that the loan of land by a chief to a subject is open to abusive manipulation by a chief who seeks to represent a formal allocation as in fact no more than a loan. The loan of land between subject and subject, however, is in a different category. In these cases, a consideration is nearly always involved, except where the purpose of the loan is to maintain title during the land-holder's absence or to provide for dependant kin while the land-holder makes his living differently or elsewhere. All such loans, however, require the consent of the chief or headman who administers land in the area. Where a consideration is involved, this can take many forms. One land-holder, for example, lent part of his land to a member of a nearby village in exchange for driving lessons. In other cases, a straight payment of cash or the setting-off of a debt is involved. Such transactions are not legal, however, if they involve the effective transfer of rights in land (or to use land) in exchange for a consideration in money or commodities.[14] But the issue is not, in fact, always so simple, since there are many arrangements, notably share-cropping, whereby what is transferred is a right to part or whole of the *produce* of land. Moreover, what is obtained in return for this, by the land-holder, is frequently the use of a plough, of oxen, of labour or of a tractor, without some or all of which the land could not be cultivated at all. There is no real discontinuity between the widely-found and quintessentially traditional practice of co-operating in land use on the one hand and entrepreneurial share-cropping on the other. It would be quite misleading to suggest that Basotho subsistence cultivators were given to mutual co-operation in any general way: rather the reverse. Essentially, the different households tend to perceive their socio-economic situation as 'zero-sum', in such terms that one man's gain is regarded as almost inevitably bound to be another's loss. But *particular* relationships of co-operation the widespread and institutionalised, operating sometimes on a neighbourly basis but more frequently on a basis of agnatic or cognatic ties, or on those of affinity. Some less structured forms of co-operation between wider groups also occur; a man can announce a *letsema*, or work party, for hoeing or harvesting, in return for which he will provide food and beer, and sometimes cash. But ploughing arrangements are generally more particularistic. They may take the unilateral form of a son ploughing for his widowed mother, or a man helping his daughter-in-law during her husband's absence. A man may lend out his stock on a long-term basis (*mafisa*), and accept assistance in ploughing in return. Two or more households, none of whom may have sufficient oxen separately, may have enough together, and arrange to plough each other's lands in turn. Unequal contributions may be paid for in cash, in kind, or by rendering other agricultural services at another date. At this point, the economic inequality of the partners begins to make itself felt in the distribution of the product, and there is an analytical progress from this arrangement to a more openly exploitative relationship between the parties. Full share-cropping can mean that a man with lands but no means of ploughing them and (for any reason such as recent arrival, unpopularity or dearth of kin) no accessible sources of co-operation, and no cash to hire a ploughman, is obliged to enter into an arrangement with an entrepreneur, whereby the latter ploughs the lands and takes half the produce. The typical entrepreneur has lands of his own, and owns or hires a tractor, using it to acquire shares in a considerable number of fields, both inside and also outside his own ward. Rural entrepreneurs are thus able to build up large *de facto* land-holdings, the nominal land-holder sometimes being little more than an unpaid labourer on his own fields. This development in effect sidesteps the customary law of land tenure. It cannot be said to be consistent with it, since it presupposes a form of social structure and a pattern of social and economic organisation of a kind entirely inconsistent with those that underlie customary law; yet it is not specifically in breach of any particular and definable provision. Little is known about the scale and total impact of these entrepreneurial arrangements in the nation as a whole. They tend to be somewhat invisible, since people do not reveal them freely, and the structure of systematic statistical inquiry is not well adapted to uncover them, much less to identify the point at which a basically co-operative if unequally balanced relationship yields to a commercial and entrepreneurial one. Nevertheless, this account indicates that the actual structure of control of land resources cannot always be read off from the general norms or even the explicit rules of customary law.

Land deprivation

Land allocation can be regarded as involving the diffuse 'right of avail'. No specific claim, in principle, exists such that a particular man can call on a particular chief to allocate him a particular land. Land deprivation, on the other hand, is specific and particular, since here a particular man is losing a particular field at the hands of a particular chief. Again, land may be allocated to or withheld from an applicant for general or negative reasons: 'there is no land, you are not my subject, there are others with a prior claim, I will see . . . come back next year.' But land can be lawfully taken away only on positive and specific grounds. The basic ground is that a 'remover' (*mofalali*) forfeits his rights automatically. As we have seen, death counts as removal,[15] but simple physical absence does not, title being without any question maintained by a wife or son, but also in many cases by more distant agnates or other kin. Removal includes or overlaps with the concept of allegiance. Except in rather special circumstances that have no bearing on the issue of principle, a man cannot hold lands under two different chiefs or headmen. If he attempts to do so, he stands to forfeit one or other or even both of his holdings. Removal and dual allegiance strike at the basis of land-holding by undermining the links between political allegiance, residence and access to arable resources.[16]

The incidence of forfeiture for non-cultivation is difficult to assess. As in most land-disputes, the case usually becomes visible only when a man finds another ploughing his land, and the issue turns on whether the chief had properly reallocated it to the interloper. In many cases, removal and non-cultivation go together, but the point does not, in the nature of the case, cause a dispute, unless the remover returns and claims his lands again.

Deprivation on the grounds that a man has more than is sufficient to maintain his household (*lelapa*) rests on the underlying norm that *mobu ke oa sechaba* (land belongs to the nation) and is in principle available for the sustenance of all. What is 'sufficient' depends partly on the size of the *lelapa*, and this in turn is partly a function of its phase in the developmental cycle. If a bachelor has any right to land at all, and the point, as has been seen, is controverted, he would not be given more than one or two. A married man, especially when he sets up his own establishment and has a child, will if he is lucky receive the 'ideal' three, and if he is a polygamist may look for more again, as he may also do if, though monogamous, he has many dependants. But if those dependants include sons, then as they grow and marry, the allocation to the household head will be in effect to the adult sons. As we have seen, there is often an area of confusion here, between the father's 'private allocation' to his son and the 'public' aspect of allocation by the chief. When the household head dies, his widow retains her land rights, but she is liable to lose one of the ideal three, two being now considered sufficient for her needs. In fact, she is often left with only one, and in some cases is hard put to it to cultivate even that, unless she enters into some co-operative or share-cropping arrangement of the kind that has been discussed earlier.

A general feature of the right to deprive a man of his surplus lands is that it can mean that a man who by hard work and good husbandry increases the yield of his holding may be penalised by forfeiting one of his lands. (Sandra Wallman also discusses these fears, 1969: 108f.) The problem is up to a point recent in origin, since it is only since improved agricultural methods have become more widely available that any qualitative difference in yield could be achieved by those able to take advantage of them. The tiny class of 'progressive farmers' certainly insist on protection against eviction or forfeiture on grounds of surplus, and also lose no time in fencing their fields against neighbouring cattle. But such farms are very rare,[17] and not altogether approved of by many chiefs.[18] Different considerations apply to ordinary subsistence cultivators. A man who does particularly well risks becoming the object of envy or witchcraft accusations, and in any case will immediately become the prey of less prosperous or unluckier kin; and he will not be able to obtain more lands for these, since what he has 'suffices' for subsistence.

Many of these grounds of deprivation leave much room for actual or felt injustice, and much more scope for manipulation by chiefs and land-issuers. Land-disputes often reveal a situation where a man has quite simply been deprived of his land, but where he can find no witnesses willing to speak to his title to it. The uncertainty surrounding what it is that counts as 'removal' and the question of how many lands are in fact 'sufficient' means that the judicial courts are often disposed to leave the matter in the hands of the chief if no compelling evidence can be found. It is also the fact, of course, that when a chief takes a land away from one man and gives it to another, he automatically acquires an ally in the new beneficiary. The loser has a fight on his hands against both his chief and his supplanter, a state of affairs that has been aggravated by the insistence, on procedural grounds, of the Judicial Commissioner's Court that an aggrieved person must sue the alleged interloper and not the chief (though the latter or his land-issuers may of course be the principal witnesses).

The security which the rules laid down in the *Laws of Lerotholi* appear to offer is thus deceptive.[19] Land-holders do not feel secure, and their feeling is amply justified. The judicial courts tend to accept the evidence of the chief, and the chances that a correct decision is eventually arrived at are probably, in the circumstances, no more than even. On the whole, the Basotho courts have a tradition of being more willing to act in the matter themselves, either by making an allocation or directing a chief to make one—in fact, *to do what they hold the chief should have done*—but there is no consistency in their practice in recent years, and they have increasingly tended to conform themselves to the received view of the judicial courts, that administrative matters are for the chieftainship. They have thus no way of getting behind the chief's 'discretion' and, except where there has been a demonstrable illegality, no attempt or desire to do so.

Land is thus open to bold and illegal initiatives, and frequently the success of a man's bid to take a field depends on the determination of his rival to defend himself. Throughout Lesotho, land-disputes are very frequent, and often the real test is whether a man will stand up for himself. Reallocations are often quite openly illegal, but they will succeed if the aggrieved person is too weak or too confused or too fearful to act. The chief may not take a hand in the matter if nothing is done about it; and if he takes the interloper's side, his opponent is obliged to go to the judicial courts, where there are fees to pay and possible costs to incur if he is unsuccessful. The invader counts on this, and feels that he has little to lose and a land to gain if events go his way.

Quasi-inheritance of land

A corollary of the rule that the land of Lesotho belongs to the nation is that other and more specific maxim that 'land is not an inheritance' (*ts'imo hase lefa*).[20] In this maxim, the word for 'land' (*ts'imo*) has a narrower reference than the word *mobu* in the wider rule. *Ts'imo* (plural *masimo*) refers specifically to arable land, and the import of the saying is that such land cannot be inherited; it does not form part of the estate (the *lefa*) that was discussed in the preceding chapter; it is not even in the same category as the garden and building sites which have been mentioned above, and which we shall examine more closely presently. The maxim that land is not an inheritance stresses the principle that death counts as removal, so that when a land-holder dies, his lands fall back to the chieftainship for reallocation. It is true that certain rights attach to any widows or minor sons that are left, and in a looser sense to any major sons too; but the maxim in question is not concerned with this qualification, but restates in the sharpest form the particular application to the case of arable land of the basic rule that all the soil of Lesotho (*mobu*) belongs to the nation. Although, as we shall see, the Basotho courts regularly rely upon the maxim, it received particular attention from the court of the Judicial Commissioner. In his judgment in a

case that has become known as '*Ma-Dyke* (Ax), Mr W. G. S. Driver
found in the doctrine that land is not an inheritance an escape from
any substantive inquiry into the lawfulness or otherwise of any claims
to land that did not fall within the specific clauses in the *Laws of
Lerotholi* protecting widows, dependants and minor sons. These
protective clauses were placed in a different juristic universe from the
other subsections where reference is made to the priority which
chiefs are supposed to accord to the adult sons and other kin of the
deceased land-holder, and *a fortiori* from the other customary
requirements governing allocation to applicants generally. All these
cases were held to fall, quite simply, within the rule that land is not
an inheritance, and the courts left the decision to the 'administrative
discretion' of the chief. The written judgment in '*Ma-Dyke* was
duplicated, and copies were circulated to the Presidents of all the
Basotho courts—a very exceptional procedure, indicative of the
importance that was attached to Mr Driver's judicial opinion in the
case.

The difficulty here is that it is true *both* that land is not an inheritance but reverts to the chieftainship for reallocation, *and* that
a son has a legitimate expectation to be given his father's lands (or
some of them, or equivalent lands), and this expectation, moreover,
is recognised in customary law. The effect of '*Ma-Dyke* was once
more to polarise the law into a judicial aspect that can be enforced
in specific terms, and an administrative aspect that is left to the
'discretion' of the chief. This fails to reflect the delicacy and subtlety
of the customary situation, in which both norms involved (the non-
inheritance of land, and the legitimacy of an heir's claims) are
maintained, without the one being sacrificed to the other or the two
being institutionally, procedurally and juristically separated into
distinct categories of right. The norms remain at a high level of
generality, and it is when they come to be applied to a particular
case that they are disposed, weighted and manipulated in such a way
as to procure a result which appears to the *lekhotla* (court in the
Sotho sense) to be the correct and lawful one.

It is true that the Basotho courts have always been ready to use the
maxim, and true also that, at least since '*Ma-Dyke*, they have
tended to move strongly to a 'judicial' view of their function. But
until modern pressures constrained them, they used the maxim,
where they did, as just one weapon in their juristic armoury among
many, not as a way of consigning a wide range of matters to an

'administrative discretion' that was not, of course, in any case institutionally segregated from other aspects of the traditional *lekhotla's* task.

One illuminating case occurred in 1948 (before *'Ma-Dyke*) (Ay). Mafetoa was a minor chief whose younger brother, Mothebesoane, lived in another ward. Mafetoa gave his brother some land to support himself and his children. Both brothers died, and were succeeded by their sons. Masopha took back the land from his cousin-brother, who went to law to reclaim it. The Paramount Chief's Court awarded the land to Mpiti; it had been given to his father for the children's support, and Mpiti had now taken his father's place as his successor; and (added the court) 'it is difficult for us to undo what your fathers had agreed on together'. The court is here seen acting *as it believed Chief Masopha should have acted*, and ignores the rule that land is not an inheritance. The Judicial Commissioner, on appeal, simply relied

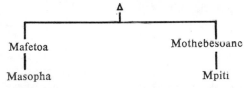

FIGURE 9   Mafetoa *v.* Mothebesoane

on the maxim and restored the land to Masopha. In another case, long after *'Ma-Dyke*, the court first agreed that land was not an inheritance, but went on to instruct the chief: 'There is your subject — attend to his plea for his children. . . . Chief, these are your children, see to them and give them lands when they come humbly before you. . . . They live with you and help you and work for you, . . .' (Ac). Of course, on appropriate occasions, the courts applied the maxim quite strictly. Where a man was confirmed in his father's lands, ploughed them for eight years and then abandoned them for ten before returning to claim them back from the man to whom they had been allocated in the interim, the Paramount Chief's Court simply quoted the maxim and dismissed the claim: 'Land is soil (*ts'imo ke mobu*), it is not an inheritance like animals or goods. When someone dies or removes, it belongs to the chief alone' (Cu). But it is wrong to suppose that the Basotho Courts traditionally regarded themselves as *constrained* by the maxim; they would use it when it served the ends the court sought to achieve, but they could turn to other and in a sense competing principles emphasising the rightful

claims of successors and the responsibility of the chieftainship when
these appeared to be neglected. 'You are the chief of orphans, but
today I see that you are their destroyer' (Ai), the Paramount Chief's
Court told a chief, and reversed his allocation; and again, 'You are the
protector of widows and orphans, and I have found that you have
betrayed your duty and used the powers you possess wrongly' (At).

Litigants regularly base their claims on their status as successors to
a deceased, and this often slips over into a claim to inherit. Sometimes, this represents little more than a daring initiative, almost
certainly foredoomed to failure. Thus, in one case, a defendant
asserted: 'This land was ploughed by my father in 1962 and I
ploughed it in 1963 after his death. It was never allocated to me.
Lands in Lesotho are an inheritance.' But he did not mean this
seriously; on appeal, when he had clearly lost, he confessed that
'lands are not an inheritance' and sought only to have the damages
reduced (Cj). As we have seen, Basotho will often try their chances
in litigation and admit subsequently that they had no real case. (The
popular proverb, 'he who stumbles in court cannot be prosecuted',
covers a multitude of such sins.) But in other cases, a claim to land
based on a right of inheritance is more soberly and responsibly
advanced. In one such case, the plaintiff said, 'This land was my
father's. There is nothing surprising in my ploughing my father's
land after he is dead. My father gave it to me. I insist that it is my
inheritance' (Bv). In another case, a plaintiff claimed land as an
inheritance on behalf of his widowed mother, acting in his capacity
as her guardian (Ch). This is a transitional case, containing an
ambivalence round which an argument can pivot. As we have seen,
there is a complex relationship between widows and heirs in respect
of property that is certainly an inheritance (cattle, money, goods);
and it is also clear that widows have an undoubted *right* (even in the
terms of the judgment in '*Ma-Dyke*) to at least a part of their
deceased husband's lands. Thus, the son, on behalf of his mother,
claims as heir and guardian in respect of what is not an inheritance but
none the less is an asset to which the widow has an enforceable title.

A case that arose in the late 1950s is of particular interest (Db),
both for the quasi-inheritance of land and for the light it throws on
the behaviour of the courts under the impact of the only half-
understood doctrine in '*Ma-Dyke*. Pius, the son of a remover who
had forfeited his lands to the chieftainship, sought to reclaim his
father's holding from Thipane, the son of the now deceased allottee

who had been awarded the lands after their forfeiture. For reasons of internal ward politics that are not relevant here, the chief with immediate jurisdiction took Pius's side and ordered Thipane to surrender the lands. Thipane took the matter to the superior chief, who reversed his subordinate's allocation and awarded the lands to Thipane again, on the grounds that 'it used to belong to his late father.' (This, of course, he was fully entitled to do; indeed, the grounds for his decision show the correct operation of his chiefly 'discretion', and are supported by the *Laws of Lerotholi*.) Pius then took the matter to the courts. The Basotho Court of first instance restored the lands to Pius, advancing as one of their principal grounds for so doing the assertion that the superior chief, in awarding the lands to Thipane for the reasons stated, had treated land as an inheritance. This is an illuminating example of how some Basotho court presidents have grossly misinterpreted the rule, and indeed wholly misunderstood what the Judicial Commissioner was saying in *'Ma-Dyke*. To rebuke the chief for attending to the fact that Thipane was his father's son was to misconceive the issue, since it was precisely the intention of *'Ma-Dyke* that the chieftainship, in its 'administrative' capacity, should have a free hand in its 'discretion'. The view taken by the Basotho Court was, in effect, that the 'administration' must act randomly and without adherence to principle, for only so could it avoid the charge that it was making land an inheritance, and importing 'judicial' criteria into 'administrative' concerns. We shall find other examples of this kind of distortion in the following chapter; it is the consequence of the polarisation of decision-making into 'judicial law' on the one hand and 'discretionary power' on the other, and the imposition of this dichotomy on to an 'executive law' system to which it is quite foreign.

It should be clear that it is no part of this argument to deny or belittle the validity, in Sotho law, of the maxim that land is not an inheritance. It is a cardinal principle of the law, and underpins the whole fabric of land use and administration. But, as with all customary principles, it cannot be considered in isolation from other norms, much less relied on as a rule of thumb that enables claims to land to be consigned to an 'administrative discretion' falling outside normative control. The institutional separation of what are now called administrative and judicial courts has the effect of placing the claims of successors and the rights of widows or minors into different and discontinuous categories, the one marked by 'power' and the other by 'law', whereas in customary terms there is no comparable discontinuity. The cases that have been discussed, and the general account of Sotho land-tenure that preceded them, suggest that over the whole area of land law there is a play of norms, general in character, potentially inconsistent in their implications, and that it is in the specification and application of these norms in particular cases that decisions are reached which are at once *unconstrained* and at the same time *lawful*.

Sites and gardens

If land is (in the qualified sense we have just discussed) clearly not an inheritance, and if certain other resources such as cattle and money as clearly are, sites and gardens form something of a mid-case. As the *Laws of Lerotholi* put it, 'on the death of a person who has been allocated the use of land for the growing of vegetables . . . or for planting . . . trees, or for residential purposes, the heir, or in the absence of the heir, the dependants of the deceased . . . shall be entitled to the use of such land so long as he or they continue to dwell thereon.'

The typical case concerns residential sites, and most attention will be given to these. Like lands, sites are a matter for allocation by the chief. To qualify, a man must bear allegiance to the chief (or headman) of the village or place where he seeks a site. If he betrays this allegiance, he forfeits his rights of residence, and therefore his site, though he is entitled to take away at least part of his hut or huts when he leaves. Removal results in forfeiture, as with lands, but again like lands, title can be derivatively maintained through close kin, including affines; and there is no obligation corresponding to the duty to cultivate. Unless a garden has been abandoned by its owners, it remains with them even if they do not make use of it. Nor can it be taken away from them simply because it is more than is 'sufficient for their subsistence'.

There is some doubt about the requirement that a man must bear allegiance to the chief of the area in which the site he inherits is located. This rule would be inequitable where buildings are irremovable and of considerable financial value, as today they so often are. Governmental protection to cover such cases is being extended, since the traditional law is clearly appropriate only where sites and buildings have little or no commercial value.

Profounder issues of principle were raised in a case where a woman claimed rights over two sites (Bq). One of these sites had been allocated to her directly; she inherited the other from her father-in-law. The chief defended his action, admitting that he had taken one of the gardens away from the woman, but pointing out that sites in the village were in very short supply. The plaintiff had already been allocated a site of her own, and should not be allowed to keep two when there were many people lacking sites who wanted one. The Basotho court of first instance supported the chief in his action, pointing out, further, that the plaintiff was not a 'dependant' of her late father-in-law, at least since she had been given a site of her own. On the father-in-law's death, the site reverted to the chieftainship for reallocation. The first Basotho court of appeal, however, reversed the decision, making the point that 'a garden is not a land (*ts'imo*)', and that the rules governing 'lands' could not be applied to it. Although it was certainly undesirable that one person should be able to accumulate a plurality of gardens and sites, this did not constitute a reason, in law, for depriving the plaintiff of her inheritance. The case then came before a third Basotho court, and here the president delivered an interesting judgment. In his view, the rule that land in a general sense (*mobu*) is not an inheritance extended to cover a case of the present kind, not precisely in the same way that it covered arable lands (*masimo*), but in terms rather of the general social and economic interests of the nation or community at large; in support, he referred to a passage in the *Laws of Lerotholi* where reference is made to 'land required in the public interest' as constituting an exception to the normal rule that deprivation is lawful only in cases of removal, death, surplusage and non-cultivation. The chief, the court said, 'was applying a benefit for the people, rather than for one person who would have several gardens to himself . . . [he has] the right to allocate the soil (*mobu*) . . . and so much the more if he applies this law for the benefit and well-being of the people'. The court also implied that the provision requiring that the occupant should 'dwell' on the site, while clearly not strictly applicable to a garden, meant that one person could not use more than one site, especially if there were a shortage of sites. This is an example of how a Basotho court can consider the norms of law at a high level of generality, applying them in a particular case but not restricting them or narrowing them on the basis of previous decisions. (It is not unusual to find that the lower court takes a stricter view of its 'judicial' function, since some

presidents have been more successfully exposed to the legal forma-
tion introduced by the colonial administration of justice than others,
and their distribution among the various Basotho courts follows no
set pattern.) When this case was appealed to the Judicial Commissioner, that court held that 'to dwell thereon' meant only that the
claimant must live 'under the chief or headman' of the area in which
the garden was located; and that 'public interest', in the *Laws of
Lerotholi*, referred to communal assets such as schools, hospitals or
roads, not to the needs of other private individuals or households.
He accordingly upheld the appellant's right to inherit the garden.

However, in spite of the doubts that were raised in this special
case of multiple ownership, sites and gardens have a greater security
than *masimo*. This is partly because it is obviously much more
difficult for a chief to reallocate a site unlawfully if people are
actually living on or near it, but also because forfeiture cannot take
place, even lawfully, except on the special conditions of removal or
possibly, as seen, where ownership of several sites is involved. Moreover, not only a son but also an heir can claim. Thus, a brother can
inherit a site, if he is heir (*mojalefa*) to the deceased.

Sites can be alienated, but since the newcomer requires an allocation, this means that the chief must agree. Whereas in a loan of land
between subjects no consideration should pass, it is not unlawful to
sell a house-property. It is not, strictly, the site but the building that
is sold, but in fact such transactions are treated very much like a sale
of land, except that, as stated, the chief's consent must be obtained.
Residential title is in fact the foundation title for all other rights,
and the chief cannot be required to allow a newcomer to acquire it
without his approval. But it is also a need even more basic than the
need for lands, and is more easily granted, since it is easier to find a
space for a hut or two than to find an unoccupied field. Similarly,
while to forfeit lands is a serious loss, to forfeit residence is more
serious still, and indeed carries the loss of lands with it. Of course,
the fact that a particular man does not inherit a site does not mean
that he loses his rights as a villager and subject; but the fundamental
character of residence helps to explain why it is less easily lost and
more securely protected than rights over arable land.

We are now in a position to come back to the concept of 'ownership'
in Sotho law, and to construct a scale along which the various rights
more or less corresponding to this concept can be ranged. At one

end of this scale are the *maboella*, in the sense of grazing grounds, which are open to all members of the entitled community and not allocated to individuals or households as such. Rights over this category of *leboella* are the furthest removed from ownership. Next, there are the other objects of chieftainship administration (*liremo*) such as thatching-grass, reeds and public trees; these are communal resources until they are subjected to specification by individuals (or individual households), whereupon those who take the produce with the chief's permission acquire an exclusive right—so long as they are resident within the ward—to the particular objects which they have cut or plucked and taken to their own use (*fructuum separatio* in Roman law parlance). Next after the *leboella* come (arable) 'lands' (*masimo*), which again are 'of the nation' until specified, but which (rights of stover apart) are more individual still. Whereas no rights are acquired over, e.g. reed-beds, but only over the reeds, and indeed only over them when they are cut, it is otherwise with lands; exclusive even if defeasible rights over arable land are acquired, and the crops belong to the landholder without *fructuum separatio* or *fructuum perceptio*. Next along the scale we can locate dwelling-sites and gardens, where title, though still defeasible, is less easily lost than in the case of lands, and where rights can pass to an heir or (with the chief's consent) be alienated for value. Finally, there are rights over those goods which are included under the notion of *lefa*, inheritance. Of these, it is possible to say that they are in a meaningful sense 'owned' As we have seen, however, even in the case of *lefa*, it is usually impossible to point unequivocally to any individual titular of a right *in rem*. As we saw in the matter of widows and heirs, the rights are best regarded as *in personam* where individuals are concerned, and rights *in rem* as attached to the agnatic lineage as a corporation.

5 Chiefs and the courts

Lesotho is famous throughout Southern Africa for the number of its chiefs. At a time when the total population was estimated to be about 800,000 (including absentees), the number of gazetted chiefs alone was rather over 1,100. But there are something in the order of 5,000 villages or hamlets where the headman receives the title of chief, and many sons of chiefs also affect or are accorded the style. However, this proliferation of chiefs should not obscure the sharp hierarchical stratification within the chieftainship. The twenty-two Principal and Ward Chiefs are in a very special category, and of the remainder, only about one hundred can be considered major chiefs on any realistic criterion.[1] The number of chiefs of substantial position is thus fairly small. The Basotho use the title *morena* (chief) very freely, and have little use for any formal terms distinguishing one grade of chieftainship from another except in contexts where such discrimination is necessary. Not only is the term *morena* used to those who are not seriously considered to be chiefs, but the ordinary form of address to a man—*ntate*—is used to those who clearly are chiefs, including the Paramount Chief himself. The relatively unstructured character of 'chieftainship terminology' should not, however, be allowed to obscure the keen consciousness of differentiation of rank with which Basotho view the hierarchy. Though they use the title *morena* rather loosely, this is no indication of any substantive looseness in their view of actual chiefs.

There is no traditional term specifically applied to the Paramount Chief, or King. He is simply *morena e moholo*, the great chief. (In modern times, the formal title of *Motlotlehi*, 'he who deserves praise', has been introduced as his official Sesotho title.) The verb *ho rena* means 'to be rich, not to work; to be a chief'.[2] The abstract noun, *borena*, formed from the same stem, means 'chieftainship, government, authority', but it shades off into a collective sense and can refer to the chieftainship as a body or corporation. The 'chieftainship' in this latter sense has, in fact, a collegiate character, in which the Paramount Chief has a pre-eminent and archetypal role, but which he does not exhaust.

There is no real term for 'non-chief' complementary to 'chief'. There is a word *mofo* which can be translated as 'commoner'; but it does not really designate a 'man who is not a chief'. Just as 'chief' implies a positively high status, so does *mofo* imply a positively low one, and has connotations of the order of 'subject', 'servant' or 'slave'. The only word that can be used without any offence would be the ordinary word for a 'person'—*motho* (plural, *batho*), as in *marena le batho ba Lesotho*, 'the chiefs and people of Lesotho' (cf. the English 'officers and men', 'master and man'). This usage can be compared with the discussion of 'ownership' and 'mastery' in Chapter 3. There are few simple, neutral terms in the hierarchical conscious-ness of traditional Sotho society.

Basotho have traditionally accorded great respect to chiefs and most continue to do so.[3] They tend to regard chieftainship as a mark of tribal self-respect and to look with pity and contempt on a man without a chief; and it is, as we have seen, a fact that Lesotho has developed both politically and administratively on the basis of chieftainship. Chieftainship is, in fact, a national institution with which Basotho often identify themselves and of which they are proud. They also, of course, recognise the unadorned political and tenurial reality of the institution, so that a man is wise to show respect to the chief of his area, no matter what his private sentiments may be.

Chiefs are assumed to be, as they often are, richer than commoners; traditionally, this implied that a subject should not rival his chief in riches. This was especially true of cattle, the principal form of wealth. Cattle are particularly associated with chieftainship. A traditional greeting to a chief is simply, 'Those cattle!' (*'Khomo tseo!'*) and indeed chiefs had almost a monopoly of owning them. One proverb runs, 'The cow lows in the chief's kraal, she is out of place in the hamlets.' Chiefs would lend their cattle out to subjects on a long-term or indefinite basis (*ho fisa*), retaining ownership of the beasts and their progeny but allowing the borrower to use the milk and dung and usually to keep the carcases of animals that died naturally. A subject with a herd so large that it might excite the jealousy and enmity of the chief or his neighbours would also lend out part of his herd in the same way, and thus give the appearance of having very few cattle in his possession.[4] Chiefs, on the contrary, are proud of their herds, and large numbers change hands in chiefly marriages. The ideal norm of a commoner marriage is twenty head, but these are usually paid in instalments, and often other animals, or cash, are substituted for cattle; chiefly bridewealth is ideally fifty head, and these should consist of actual stock and be paid in one delivery.

Chiefly wealth is often real enough in modern times too, and several Principal Chiefs are moderately rich men by any standard. But whereas there was little that could be done with traditional wealth except, in the famous phrase, to use it to build up 'social capital', chiefs have other outlets for their money today. Moreover, since their revenues are now largely independent of the communities over which they rule, fewer popular sanctions can be mobilised against their defection from the traditional chiefly virtues, exaggerated though these may be in contemporary consciousness. Of course, chiefs have always lived better than their subjects, but in the past the difference was one of degree rather than of kind. They ate meat more often, their huts were larger and better supplied, and above all they had more wives; but there was no radical discontinuity between their general manner of life and that of most of their subjects.

Demographic changes have also played an important part in changing the relationship between chiefs and people. As we have seen, it was possible in the past for people to move from one chief to another, and in the early days of expansion there was even some competition among chiefs to secure followers. The increase in population and the greater pressure on land resources have critically altered the balance of power in the chiefs' favour.[5] These developments have coincided with and been partly shaped by the rise of a modern political consciousness (the best accounts are in Halpern 1965, Spence 1968 and Weisfelder 1969, 1972a, 1972b). The general effect of this has been to render the chieftainship, in one aspect still the unique and 'total' governing institution in the nation, in another aspect no more than one limited group competing with other groups that are structurally equal to and co-ordinate with it; this has obvious implications for its continued legitimacy and for its claims to represent a 'national' as against a partial and partisan interest.

But although many subjects have lost their 'actuarial', they have retained their 'moral' expectations of their chiefs. The ideal chiefly virtues which are looked for are those of generosity, fatherliness, hospitality and (much more ambivalently) strength. A well-known riddle or proverb points to several such qualities: 'What is a tree on which all birds sit?—It is a chief.' A chief is expected to give rest, shelter and hospitality to all, and to be strong enough to support the many who depend on him.[6] We saw in the last chapter how the Paramount Chief's Court regularly recalled chiefs to their obligations when they neglected their responsibilities to their subjects, more especially to orphans and widows. One accused person relied on these general conceptions of chiefly duties to justify his refusal to join in the work of ploughing the chieftainship fields. 'I work and yet he does not feed me. . . . It is only right that when he issues a call to the work-party he should give us food. . . . A chief should feed his people.' Although in this case the Paramount Chief's Court did not support the defendant, the cry 'I work and yet he does not feed me' is eloquent of the reciprocities that he saw to be involved (Bp).

The might of chieftainship, its greater strength than the strength of ordinary people, though it enables chiefs to bear the weight of so many social responsibilities, is more ambivalent in its moral value. Most proverbs and sayings that reflect this aspect of chieftainship have a cynical or else a menacing ring. 'The word of a chief builds a kraal' (the chief's word is powerful and must be obeyed), 'the chief is a hornless cow' (*viz.*, he is unpredictable and capricious); 'the chief's arm has a long reach'; 'the chief does not put in the second blow, he is the killer' (a chief gets credit for and the profit from what his subjects do). Here we see reflected that ambivalent quality in all domination or *Herrschaft* which was noticed in the first chapter. But while Basotho are sensitive to and critical of the shortcomings of chiefs—indeed, it would be impossible for them not to be aware of them—they tend still to regard these deficiencies as precisely the *abuses* of an office that is still, in its essence, worthy of respect. Just as fraudulent witchdoctors do not destroy belief in authentic practitioners, so selfish and irresponsible chiefs do not destroy respect for authentic chieftainship.

Chiefs constitute the network whereby the government and administration of the country are carried on. The Paramount Chief communicates with the whole nation by sending letters or messengers to the Principal and Ward Chiefs, who then pass the information or instruction to their subordinate chiefs, and so on down the hierarchy until each village and homestead has received it. Modern government also makes extensive use of the chieftainship, and in fact could hardly function without it. The normal link is through the Department of Local Government, which communicates with Principal Chiefs and through them with their subordinates. District Commissioners also communicate with their districts through the chiefs. No other serviceable form of local administration yet exists. The District Councils that were established in 1948 were, in spite of subsequent reforms, less than effective. The one-time Native Tax, later Basuto Tax, is also collected through the chiefs, and many Basotho regularly describe their allegiance in terms of the chief through whom the tax is paid. Chiefs are also both empowered and required to act as law enforcement officers throughout most of the country, making use both of their traditional right to have their orders obeyed ('lawful orders', in modern practice), and of their more recent power to prosecute offenders before the statutory courts for criminal acts (the latter, of course, including disobedience to a lawful order). They arrest and detain alleged offenders, prepare evidence and present the accused before the judicial court for prosecution. Chiefs thus act as the representatives of their local communities to higher authority and as representatives of higher authority to their people; in Lesotho as elsewhere, they are therefore deeply implicated in the 'predicament of the modern African chief' (Fallers 1955) and suffer the familiar discomforts of their dilemma.

Traditionally, every chief had his own court. There was no distinction between what are now called 'administrative' and 'judicial' affairs.[7] The chief discharged a plurality of tasks, which were not segregated into distinct 'roles' or 'capacities'. He acted as judge in disputes between his subjects, he adjudicated rival claims to land, he allocated land to applicants and withdrew it from those who had forfeited their right to enjoy it; he maintained order in his ward and punished those who broke it; he issued instructions to his subjects, presided over the popular assembly or *pitso*, called on his people to labour in his fields, appropriated the fines paid to him in court and witnessed all the major and many of the minor events and transactions in his ward; he was spokesman for his people in a question with another area or with a higher chief, and he transmitted the policies and directives of his superiors back to his people. In all these various activities, the chief was performing, not a variety of roles, but the one, unitary role of 'being a chief'. In important matters, an aggrieved subject could complain to a higher chief, as far as his prudence or perseverance permitted him to go in the hierarchy.

We have already discussed (Chapter 2 above) the proliferation of wards which the expansion of the chieftainship and the system of 'placings' gave rise to in the 1920s and 1930s. Since every chief had a court—and valued it for the revenues which it represented—there existed a bewildering variety of jurisdictions that came, in the end, to make the efficient and equitable administration of justice virtually impossible (at any rate, in the eyes of the confused colonial authorities). The 1938 Proclamations, whose political consequences have already been considered, laid the foundations for a revolutionary change in the structure and role of the courts. Under the new legislation, no chief could hold a court without a warrant, and each court's powers and jurisdiction were limited to what the warrant specified. The effective implementation of the Proclamations did not follow at once. All the 1,340 chiefs whose names appeared in the first official gazette (which, it will be recalled, now became the statutory charter of chiefly rights) received court warrants. This served to disguise from most Basotho the magnitude of the changes contemplated by the new laws, and in particular to obscure the basic principle that it was no longer chieftainship but administrative recognition by warrant that bestowed the authority to hold a court. The empirical situation persisted with little evident change until the end of the war. In 1946, however, warrants were issued to no more than 121 chiefs, and the figure dropped to 106 a few years later. Moreover, the new court presidents were no longer necessarily chiefs; and though chiefs were still frequently appointed as presidents, since they tended to be the best qualified people, they were as a rule deliberately appointed to courts outside their jurisdictions, and commoner presidents were not usually expected to hold a court within the ward of their own chief. Even the boundaries of the courts' jurisdictions no longer always coincided with those of the chieftainship wards. The separation of the chieftainship from the courts reached a further stage in 1958. Up to that time, the third level of the Basotho court structure had consisted of an Appeal Court (in four divisions) centred in the Paramount Chief's royal capital at Matsieng. Although, strictly speaking, this geographical location had no legal significance whatsoever, it was inevitable that most Basotho would associate the court at Matsieng with the Paramount Chief, and an element of continuity with the old system was thus maintained. In 1958, this level of appeals was abolished and the courts restructured again. In 1964, there were only fifty-six lower level courts in the country, which together with a dozen appeal courts made a total of sixty-eight. By now, the judicial system had been entirely detached from the chieftainship structure, though, as before, many chiefs were still acting as presidents of the courts. Meanwhile, a new controlling authority had been superimposed on the Basotho courts, in the form of the Judicial Commissioner, an officer of the colonial administration who had a general superintendence over the Basotho courts and acted as the highest level of appeal within the 'Native Court' structure.

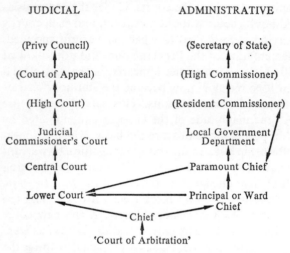

FIGURE 10   *Judicial and administrative structure*

Appeals lay, with leave, from the Judicial Commissioner to the High Court.[8] (The High Court also hears appeals from the Roman-Dutch Subordinate Courts (Magistrates' Courts) as well as being itself a court of first instance with unlimited jurisdiction. Appeals from the High Court go to the Court of Appeal and from there to the Privy Council. See figure 10.)

The 1938 legislation and its implementary sequels did not, however, apply in the same terms to what were called the 'administrative' functions of chieftainship. Specific warrants were necessary before a chief could lawfully hold a 'judicial' court, but recognition and gazettement were all that were required for a chief to exercise his administrative powers. Moreover, it was expected that chiefs would continue to carry on their administration through their courts, in much the same way as they always had done before. Two parallel systems thus came into being—the judicial structure, consisting of the Basotho courts and the Judicial Commissioner, and the administrative structure, made up as before of the chiefs and their administrative committees, or courts. The latter bore a very close resemblance to the former chiefs' courts, though now they were limited to administrative matters falling within the responsibility of chiefs as these were now regarded; all judicial matters could be dealt with only by the courts of warrant. The full effects of this segregation of function were also, of course, only felt when the Proclamations of 1938 were effectively implemented.

Fuller theoretical consideration will be given to the distinction between 'judicial' and 'administrative' in the concluding chapter, but something of its significance should be anticipated here. Basically, the judicial courts are said to be concerned with the ascertainment, declaration and (where necessary) enforcement of existing rights, at the suit of the party claiming them. The administration on the other hand is concerned with the creation, modification or extinction of rights, so far as such acts lie within the legally defined competence of the administering power. When two parties come before a judicial court, the task of the judge or president is to set about an inquiry into what the rights of the parties *are,* so far as these are relevant to the issue brought before him, and, having completed this inquiry, to declare its conclusion and embody it in a particular and enforceable decision. He cannot create rights where none existed before, nor can he extinguish or modify any right that he finds to exist. The administration, on the other hand, so long as it does not step outside its own defined area of competence or act in breach of natural justice, can create rights where there were none before, or alter an existing situation of right by modifying or extinguishing rights that had previously been enjoyed. The existing rights of parties are no more than ancillary to the administrative task; administration may weigh such rights as *one factor* in coming to its decision, but cannot properly be bound by them. We have already come across several instances of how this distinction works in practice. For instance, we have seen how the judicial courts discover a problem in handling disputes over inheritance, since when the parties come to court, they do so precisely because the 'family council' has *not succeeded* in establishing rights over the *lefa* or inheritance. The judicial courts therefore tend to look for universal rules of law enabling them to declare what the rights of the parties *are*, and naturally they find this hard to reconcile with the principle that it is for the 'family council' to create them when this is what the family have just failed to do. In matters of land tenure, too, we have seen that the judicial courts will only act where an existing right has been invaded or unlawfully taken away; where allocation is concerned, it is usually a question not of declaring but of creating a right, and the court will not interfere with this since it lies within the 'administrative discretion' of the chief. We have also seen how the institutional separation of the judicial from the administrative systems has led to a polarisation of decision-making into an essentially declaratory 'law' on the one hand and an essentially 'power-based' or 'free' discretion on the other; this was not the state of affairs under the previous system, where the customary law furnished the principles in terms of which the chief was required to carry out all his tasks, and where the dichotomy of judicial and administrative courts was both institutionally and conceptually absent.[9]

The 1938 legislation not only left essentially intact the old chiefs' courts, though limiting them to administrative functions; it also expressly permitted the existence of 'arbitration courts'—informal tribunals, without statutory powers, whose function it was to settle minor disputes if the parties were willing, or, if they failed to do so, to remit the case to a judicial tribunal for determination by a formal court. These courts of arbitration thus constitute a third element in the structure that was expected to evolve. But, in fact, the function of informal arbitration was very largely discharged by the chiefs' courts, now as before, with the result that the now supposedly 'administrative' courts took over the quasi-judicial function of arbitration. At the lower levels of structure, at least—the levels where chiefly authority was immediately visible and routinised—the judicial and administrative roles were once again largely fused.

The chieftainship and the courts of arbitration thus continue to play an important part in dispute settlement and in judicial affairs generally. The lowest level of arbitration takes place in the village, where the chief or headman, or his deputy, sits as a chief's court has always sat and together with his council of advisers attempts the resolution of every kind of issue, whether civil or criminal, judicial or administrative. From one point of view, it can be seen as a clearing house for a wide variety of matters. Those that it cannot settle—those that, in the indigenous expression, are 'too hard' (*thata*) for it —are remitted to whatever authority or court seems appropriate. There is considerable variation in the assiduity and conscientiousness displayed by minor chiefs and headmen in running the lowest level arbitration courts. Some work hard and responsibly and command the willing respect and obedience of their subjects; others are lazy, senile, venal or partisan, and if they lack the power to enforce their will, matters that come before them are likely to proceed to a further stage before settlement. This further stage is unlikely to be the judicial court. Since, as we have seen, the arbitration court of lowest rank is in fact simply the chief's court under another name, matters that are not settled there are usually taken to the court of the chief immediately superior in rank, and from him it may well proceed to another stage in the supposedly 'administrative' hierarchy too. Only then, very often, will the matter be sent to the lowest-level Basotho court; and this latter is indeed often referred to, in local parlance, as a 'court of appeal'. Such is the litigious passion of the Basotho that the judicial structure could hardly function were it not underpinned by this officially invisible hierarchy of chiefly tribunals. Even the Judicial Commissioner's Court, which before the abolition of the Appeal Courts at Matsieng was a third level of appeal, handles anything up to 500 or 600 cases a year; but since, as we have seen, there may be two or three 'informal' stages before the lowest rung of the judicial hierarchy is even reached, it is more realistic to see the Judicial Commissioner as a fifth or sixth stage in the total procedure of settlement.

In theory, every Mosotho has a legal right to initiate a civil action before the Basotho courts. But very few Basotho believe this. They believe that they cannot 'open the court' without the authority and interposition of the chief. Many clerks of court refuse to register cases unless the litigant produces a letter from his chief. This is, of course, illegal, but it is a practice connived at by both courts and chiefs; and where, as often happens, a disputant is illiterate or insufficiently literate to cope with the formal side of his case, the chief and the arbitration court can perform an essential function in helping him to complete the official procedures and prepare himself for the hearing.

Once the case is before the court, the chief's responsibilities do not end. He should make sure that witnesses are cited, and he should be told of the decision reached by the court so that he may be sure that its terms are understood and its decision followed through. In criminal matters, his evidence is often the decisive element in the case, and he is frequently an important witness in civil actions as well, not least of course in matters concerning the allocation of arable land.

The role of the chiefs in the administration of justice is thus still an important one at various levels and in various ways—not all of them recognised in the formal system. But much depends on the individual chief, and on the general effectiveness of chieftainship in the local area. Where chiefs are lazy or incompetent, people will seek their justice where they can find it. There is also evidence of a growing sense that the judicial courts offer an independent set of tribunals against which even the chief cannot ultimately prevail.

The formal transformation of the old system into the new was as rapid as the authorities chose to make it, and this corresponds to the outline of the changes in court structure that have just been described. It was one of the major tasks of the Judicial Commissioner to try to translate the new system into action and to conscript the Basotho courts into the service of the 'judicial' goals now set before them. The legal interest of the twenty-five or thirty years following the first decisive moves to implement the intentions of the Proclamations lies in the evidence which this period of transition uncovers of the continuing impetus, within the new and supposedly judicial courts, of forces whose roots lie deep in the older society. Although programmes of re-education were set up and training courses for court presidents eventually instituted, 'judicial' attitudes had still not taken a firm hold at all levels of the Basotho courts, even a quarter of a century after the establishment of the Judicial Commissioner's Court. Some of the most illuminating evidence of the persistence of 'chiefly' practice within the courts is to be found in the court of the Paramount Chief (who throughout most of this period was the Chieftainess Regent, 'Mantsebo). For a long time after 1938 it remained the practice of the Paramount Chief to 'confirm' the decisions of her (judicial) court, and though this was intended by the legislators to be a mere formality, and tolerated by government as a gesture of respect to the royal office, it was not so regarded by her or (frequently) by her advisers. As late as 1945, her judicial court stated in terms that 'the Paramount Chief has the authority to cancel or confirm or alter any judgment as she sees proper' (Ar). She would also confirm a judgment and then, some years later, reverse the decision administratively (Be). Although there was some in-stitutional separation, in terms of personnel, between her judicial and her administrative courts, the Chieftainess herself believed that she equally superintended them both. Other chiefs and courts shared this view. One major chief—the head of the Molapo cardinal house —recalled the days when 'we had all powers as chief. We were free to alter any judgment' (Ca); and a Basotho court declared, in 1952, that 'there are no limits on the orders that the administration (sc., the chieftainship) can give' (Ba). In one case, the Paramount Chief's Court stopped the hearing and said: 'We do not allow this case to go on, as it causes the Chief displeasure. . . . He is a son of Lerotholi and so are we, and we naturally share the sense of grievance he has suffered in this matter' (Cp).

But it would be more than misleading to imply that every depar-ture from the judicial ideal was abusive or contrary to natural justice, as some of the examples just quoted clearly are. Most could not be reasonably so described. Sometimes, we find an approach to the rules of evidence which, while unacceptable in judicial terms, is quite appropriate to the traditional position of the chief. Hearsay evidence, for instance, is accepted if the witness is reliable. A village headman stated 'I am the chief's counsellor; I know what happened because I am the headman, and I know the village's affairs' (Bx). His indirect knowledge of events leading up to an act of arson was relied on by the court. The judge in a court of first instance made a private inquiry into the facts, and on appeal he represented the principal witness (Ac). Another judge relied on his personal know-ledge of a boundary in reaching his decision in a land-dispute (Cw). In another case, the court took cognisance of the appellant's trade as a tailor without evidence being led (Cg). These cases illustrate the limited role-differentiation of the traditional system; the judicial role is not fully segregated from the other roles—observer, actor, leader—carried by the office-holder. The courts also tend to depart from 'judicial' principles in allocating the onus of proof. Onus is not strictly apportioned and sometimes tends to lie on the defendant. The older practice was for the plaintiff simply to make his claim and invite his opponent to rebut it.[10] Talcott Parsons has shown how this procedure is consonant with the existence of 'diffuse' and 'particular-istic' relationships, the burden lying on the one who refuses a claim to produce a good reason for doing so (1954: 39). Sometimes this takes the form of the plaintiff asking the court to assess the quantum of the claim (Al). (One litigant, aware of the Judicial Commissioner's insistence on a specified claim, mocked the system by suing for £59,600 where the sum involved was about £28 (Dc).)

We have already come across examples of how the Paramount Chief's Court often ignored the distinction between judicial and administrative affairs, ordering a chief to make an allocation, for instance (Bo), or itself doing what it considered the chief should have done, directly allocating land to the persons to whom, in its view, the chief should have allocated it (Ay). In a civil action between two chiefs over the administrative title to a certain area, the court took the area in dispute away from both parties and awarded it to a third (Cx). Very often, such decisions are accompanied by homilies[11] aimed at any party in the case whom the court feels to have fallen short of his general social and moral obligations. Instances of the Paramount Chief's Court rebuking chiefs and recalling them to their duties have been cited, but all the Basotho courts engage in such instruction, nowhere more commonly than in actions between husband and wife. Thus, the lower court told one couple, 'We do not find any reason why we should divorce elderly persons like you, who should lead an exemplary life and who are about to acquire a daughter-in-law to whom you are supposed to give moral instruction. . . . Go and keep the peace and give a good example to your children' (Cl).

We have already noticed more than once that questions of inheritance present problems to the judicial courts. The Basotho courts have seldom felt inhibited, however, from taking charge of the distribution of estates, annexing to their decision, as often as not, remarks about the proper conduct expected of the principal heir in relation to the dependants left by his deceased father (Bi). The distribution of household goods between spouses is a question of the same kind, and in one case the Basotho court not only issued an order in respect of the property but threatened that if the husband did not obey, he would be deprived of his lands (Br). In cases such as these, the Judicial Commissioner, on appeal, has nearly always taken refuge in the distinction between judicial and administrative affairs (Cm). In matters of inheritance, the decision lies with the heir, and the courts are not competent to intervene. Many disputes are put aside as 'not justiciable' and either sent back to the disputants to sort out themselves or else referred to an administrative authority with whose 'free discretion' the judicial courts cannot interfere. The difference in approach of the Judicial Commissioner on the one hand, and the Basotho courts on the other, to issues of land allocation has been discussed already: for the former, the rule that 'land is not an inheritance' releases the judicial courts from their responsibility for any issue that is not a matter of a specific and enforceable pre-existing right; for the latter, there still survives the tradition whereby the chief, in exercising his 'discretion', is no less bound by the general norms of the law: and these norms are equally within the scope of the court's interest and authority. The consequence of polarising 'law' and 'discretion' is to sever the ties binding that discretion to the law, and to bring it about that, authority being 'powerless', power must in compensation lack authority. 'Discretionary' acts thus tend to be released from legal control. In one instance, this took a bizarre form, when an employee of the Basuto National Treasury at Matsieng (the royal capital) sued for wrongful dismissal and found his plea rejected by the Paramount Chief's Court on the grounds that the matter was an administrative one (Bc). It was left to the Judicial Commissioner to explain that an illegality remained actionable even though it was committed by the administration. Such a reading of the relative positions of the judicial and administrative courts is, however, not uncommon. We have already discussed the curious case of Pius and Thipane, where, it will be recalled, the chief in his administrative court awarded a land to Thipane on the grounds that it had belonged to his father (Db). This was, as we saw, not merely a 'lawful' decision in the sense of being a *competent* one, but a decision that respected the principles of succession and quasi-inheritance that underlie the law of land allocation; but the Basotho (judicial) court rebuked the chief and his court for acting as though land were an inheritance. The implication of this rebuke was that only by acting in an arbitrary way and renouncing any guiding principle in his allocation could the chief escape the charge that he was usurping the 'judicial' function. In another case again, a chief was placed virtually in the position of having to act as unjudicially as possible in order to have some assurance that his administrative decision would be upheld by the judicial courts (Cf). Sometimes, the confusion worked in the opposite direction, as when a chief acted under the impression that he could not make an administrative decision in an opposite sense to the judgment of a judicial court (Ce), but more commonly the effect of the institutional structure has been to

confine the judicial courts to an inflexible and 'legalistic' view of
their function, and to oblige the administration to act arbitrarily.[12]
The courts are inhibited from exercising the functions of equity,
while administration is stripped of the inhibitions of law.

Conclusion:
Politics, administration
and executive law

In a justly celebrated discussion, M. G. Smith has outlined a conceptual framework for the analysis of government of impressive theoretical value (1960: chapter 2). He regards 'the essential components of the structure and process of government' as being 'political' and 'administrative' activities;[1] though these two components are found in a whole range of empirical relationships and associations the one with the other, they are analytically distinct, political activities being characterised by 'power', administrative activities by 'authority'. The focus of political activities lies in the selection of policy and is marked—and defined—by contraposition. Administrative activity consists of authorised processes and lacks contraposition at any level, being an 'inherently hierarchic' type of organisation. Empirically, the two components are not found in ideal form, yet the analytical categories can be employed to describe and classify the actual systems of government that exist in the field. Smith notes that no set of administrative rules could cover every possible situation or lay down in advance the precise action that an administrative officer should take. In so far as the administrative component is thus free, and indeed obliged, to take decisions, it exercises political powers. Further, although in such cases the administration is operating within a framework of authority and exercising only derived or delegated rights, its decisions are regarded by subordinates as acts of power, as indeed they are, though circumscribed by the enabling provision. It must be added that empirically no code, as Smith notes, can of itself secure obedience and no system of supervision can wholly exclude *ultra vires* action by administrative organs or personnel. In so far as the administration is able to exceed its authority, therefore, it displays in still clearer form an exercise of power and a usurpation of political activity.

Smith's analysis does not deal explicitly with the place of law in political or government systems.[2] In a brief reference he places it among the administrative activities of government, as standing apart from the executive or political spheres; it does not, therefore, appear to involve the taking of policy decisions or the exercise of power. This corresponds to the view that the English legal system has traditionally taken of itself: its function is essentially declaratory rather than creative. No matter what hesitation, debate and uncertainty precede judgment, no matter now many inferior judgments are overturned on appeal, the court tends to regard itself not as making but as declaring law, the law itself being conceived as existing, disembodied, in some noumenal realm of pure essence, from which it realises itself with ever greater particularity and sharpness of definition as it moves from potency to act in the mouths of judges. Judges 'find the law', they do not make it. They declare that the law governing a particular circumstance 'is' so-and-so, as though even if they had, *per impossibile*, stated otherwise, it would still have been so. Even where a judgment incorporates an award of a particular sum of money in damages, this is still an act not of power but of authority; it is the ultimate self-realisation of the law, which here reaches a particularity that briefly reveals its features before it returns to the realm where only its hinder parts are seen: where the law never is, but always is to be. Jerome Frank quotes from Abbott's *Justice and the Modern Law* as follows: 'The judicial process in ascertaining or applying the law is essentially similar to the process by which we acquire our knowledge of geometry. . . . In the great majority of cases the solution of [legal problems] is as certain and exact as an answer to a problem in mathematics' (1949: 8). Blackstone writes that the judge 'is not delegated to pronounce a new law, but to maintain and expound the old one'. Even where a decision is 'most evidently contrary to reason' or divine law, 'the subsequent judges do not pretend to make a new law, but to vindicate the old one from misrepresentation. . . . It is declared, not that such a sentence was bad law, but that it was not law. . . . Our lawyers . . . with justice . . . tell us, that the law is the perfection of reason. . . . Not that the particular reason of every rule of law can at this distance of time be always precisely assigned; but it is sufficient that there be nothing in the rule flatly contradictory to reason' (1783: Book I, Introduction, Section 3: 68–71).

The myth is described by Sawer as being one of 'decision inevitability' (1965: 105; see also Moore 1970: 323). Frank (1949) analyses it as involving a notion of law as a logical plenum, and in expounding the view he is concerned to attack he writes that according to this myth, 'law is a complete body of rules existing from time immemorial and unchangeable. . . . The law, ready made, pre-exists the judicial decision. Judges are simply "living oracles" of law. They are merely "speaking law". . . .'

Such a view represents the *ultima ratio* of authority, and the total disappearance of power. It supposes a code—the 'ideal law'—wherein every possible configuration of acts and events is provided for and where every pronouncement of the administrative officer, whilst it may appear at the level of phenomena as a 'decision' and is regularly so described, is really in essence an act of pure obedience: not, of course, to an identifiable human superior, but to the law itself. Even where the court is applying the enacted law of a legislature or other sovereign, this obedience is not, strictly speaking, given to a determinate superior. The English and Scottish courts do not inquire into what that sovereign intended to enact but into what it did enact; the object of obedience remains the law, and not the person or institution that made the law. But it is no accident that, to the lawyer at least, the quintessence of law does not reside in statute but in the common law—'judge-made law', as it is often called, but 'judge-found law' as it is better termed in the context of the 'declaratory' theory of judicial functions.

The declaratory view of the judicial task also possesses the characteristic of being unverifiable; since there is by definition no alternative access to the self-existing 'law' other than the words of judges, there is no even theoretical possibility of independently ascertaining the 'truth' of the claims of the declaratory theory. In this lies both its strength and its weakness. The law embodies the values of the society, and its progressive self-realisation in 'decisions' of ever sharper particularity is the mechanism whereby it fulfils the 'regulatory' function of which Eisenstadt speaks (1959), transmitting those values to the members of the society and eliciting (or compelling) their loyalty to the total political system to which they belong.

Smith's scheme has much to recommend it. The two analytical elements of power and authority seem to define two distinguishable components in social action. and moreover to do so in a manner that is sensitive to the 'normative' or legitimate features that might be regarded, and with reason, as the defining characteristics of 'law'. But although Smith's scheme is useful for some purposes (as he himself has shown) it is only a starting point for the conceptual analysis of law. In the first place, there are certain theoretical difficulties in his way of discussing authority and power. It is perhaps more satisfactory to regard authority as one of several *bases* of power than as a special *kind* of power. This point of view has been well expressed by Parsons (1960) and admirably glossed by Giddens (1968). One particular source of confusion in Smith's approach is that if authority is seen as a special case of power, the opposition should (correctly) be between two kinds of power, *viz.*, that with and that without authority; but though the analysis may start from that point, it all too easily shifts into opposing power on the one hand to authority on the other, which in the original terms is to contrast two different levels of structure. The whole and the part are treated as co-ordinate. Again, if authority is regarded as legitimate power, there is no easy answer to the question of the source of non-legitimate power: this cannot always be, or at least cannot remain, simply force or self-interest. Moreover, when Smith's scheme is applied to actual cases, it can lead to false conclusions about the processes described. It leads to the polarisation we have noticed into 'discretion' on the one hand and 'rule-governedness' on the other, which though a fair reflection of the conceptual set of 'declaratory' legal systems, distorts the reality of what is here characterised as 'executive law'. Furthermore, the scheme is unbalanced. It implies that at one end of the continuum, the empirical correlate of (pure) 'power' would be the Hobbesian war of all against all. This is acceptable enough in itself, but the polarity is not effectively balanced by any conceivable state of society at the other end of the scale. One way of approaching this is to observe that it is impossible to frame a rule that defines its own application. A second-order rule must be invoked to define the application of the first, and a third-order rule to define that of the second, and so on, in infinite regress. The purely 'administrative' myth is conceivable only in a society where the law has no point of contact with concrete action at all: and where, in consequence, the problem of relating structure to event is eliminated by the expedient of eliminating events, and so eliminating sociology. It is, however, precisely in so far as law is the point where life and logic meet (Maitland) that it raises theoretical problems at all; therefore it is to that point, and not to points on either side of it, that any projected solutions must be directed.

Popper's sketch of a wholly 'abstract' society has many features in common with a wholly 'administrative' one (1962: 174–5); but a better example for the present purpose is that of the 'musical banks' in Samuel Butler's *Erewhon*.[3] These institutions form an entirely self-sufficient and 'perfect' system—but they have no concrete function and their absence would make no difference to Erewhon in practical terms. Butler, of course, had the church in mind, but the allegory would fit a judicial system that became wholly specialised and 'administrative'. Legal concepts properly exist on a kind of inter-level between logic and life. One of the first lessons that a student of law must learn is that many words of common usage are given a specialised juristic meaning, and become terms of art. Thus, 'negligence', 'injury', 'fault' and even 'lawful' carry heavy loads of interpretation and commentary. In some instances, special terms evolve (e.g., 'tort') which bear this technical quality in their faces, but in the majority of cases an ordinary word is adopted and given a specialised sense. But it is as important to recognise that this sense cannot be wholly specialised, if the courts are to engage with the concrete life of society at all. For example, the legal concept of 'negligence' retains much of its everyday motivation as well as its quality as a term of art, and it is exactly this 'bridging' characteristic that renders it serviceable in both 'law' and 'life'. (It was by virtue of its everyday connotations, for instance, that Lord Devlin was able to enlarge the English common law of 'negligence' in *Hedley Byrne* v. *Heller* [1964] 4 AC 465.)

It is not proposed to review here the massive literature that exists on the nature of the judicial process.[4] The 'declaratory' view which has been presented above in ideal form is not accepted by jurists of any sophistication, though in modified form it still tends to represent the official doctrine of the courts, or at least of the 'judicial folk-lore' that underlines the less academic jurisprudence of many practising lawyers and judges.[5] The existence of an efficient legislature naturally enables a form of declaratory theory to be workable, since enacted law can always be invoked to change the law as 'found' by the court. But though the 'declaratory' theory *in se* cannot be taken quite seriously by the analyst, it exists as an ethnographic fact in the legal thinking of many societies where law has not been codified.[6] Codification implies the formal exposition of the law in systematic form and is normally followed and validated by legislative enactment. Although a body of case-law grows up round the code, this '*jurisprudence*' (in the French sense) is always referred back to the code and does not as a rule take its place or stand on the same level of authority. Consequently, the Code is the ultimate 'law' and if it is of recent origin (like the codes of most modern states, which owe their existence directly or indirectly to Napoleon) it is clearly not to be expected that a quasi-mystical attitude should grow up towards it. Only where a code or *corpus* is of ancient origin does it emerge as 'Law' in the sense in which the word has been capitalised above; thus the Roman Twelve Tables were still the formal object of reverence even in the time of Justinian, when their relevance to legal and social problems had long ago vanished.[7] But where the law has not been codified, its origins cannot be determined by any particular human act to which a date can be given; it is regarded as issuing from God himself, or as having been delivered by a founding ancestor, or (rather less simply) as secreted by the society itself over immemorial time. It does not now follow that the acts and words of judges will be regarded as infallibly or by definition declaring the true law; least of all will this follow if the judges themselves are not members of the society in which they hold office; in this case, indeed, judicial activity is seen by members of the society as an act of power, both because the judge is regarded as a stranger to the Law, and because he is seen as simply one part of the alien government set over the nation; and indeed, in Lesotho, until the recent past he may well in his other roles have been a District Commissioner or other executive officer.[8] Furthermore, we have seen that following the changes imported into the court structure by the 1938 Proclamations no chief continued to act as a judge in his own ward and the number of courts was reduced in the course of a few years from over a thousand to fewer than a hundred; in consequence, courts ceased to form a natural and daily part of the ordinary Mosotho's life; such courts as continued to operate were no longer so directly associated with the local chieftainship as such, and thus ceased to be implicated in the nexus of other relationships, economic, disciplinary, political, administrative and ideological, which characterised the chieftainship in the traditional society. All this meant that the Basuto courts, like the European ones though to a lesser degree, could not be regarded as *ipso facto* the authentic exponents of the 'Law'. The very affirmation that such-and-such a decision was not 'our Law' implies the existence of this law as an entity existing apart from its expositors; and it does not need a long acquaintance with the Basotho to become aware that they regard their law as the special possession of the Sotho nation, expressive of its fundamental values and a major determinant of its identity.

The historical experience of Lesotho has given this insistence on legal identity and purity an urgency and immediacy that go further still to account for the juristic awareness and pride that mark the people. The basic principle of land-law—that the land belongs to the nation—is the charter on which the Basotho have based their resistance to white colonisation and settlement. When sovereignty inhered in the British Crown, chiefly 'ownership' of the land became a main conceptual focus of Lesotho's affirmation of a continuing if attenuated independence; since much of Sotho law is concerned with land use and administration, the will to preserve such independence as remained has stimulated an insistent loyalty to the law as such.

In his study of Soga Law, L. A. Fallers, as we saw, has defined 'legal reasoning' as 'the application to the settlement of disputes of categorising concepts that define justiciable normative issues . . . that may then be decided simply in terms of inclusion or exclusion' (1969: 32). In a later passage, he surveys the principal literature in the anthropology of law in Africa and remarks that 'there is, I think, a continuum from the less to the more legalistic legal subculture' (1969: 328). A continuous scale of 'legalism', he indicates, could be constructed, and empirical legal systems placed along it; and he ranks the Arusha (Gulliver 1963), the Tiv (Bohannan 1957), the Lozi (Gluckman 1955, 1965, etc.) and the Soga, in that order, from the least to the most 'legalistic'. For Fallers, in fact, law is a discrete variable, of which there can be 'more' or 'less'. In this he has made a major contribution to legal anthropology, by reinstating law as a specific mode of social action and showing the way back from the theoretical desert of 'social control' into which social anthropologists have tended to stray. 'The anthropological study of law', he writes, 'has, I think, suffered from a reluctance to recognise that some societies make little, if any, use of law' (1969: 11); and in terms of the definition of legal reasoning quoted above, he both declines to equate legal process with arbitration and mediation (1969: 10, 13), and pungently rejects the familiar positivism that would identify custom with law: 'Saying that custom is a *source* of law is not the same as saying that custom *is* law. . . . It is not the whole complex of rules . . . but rather a selection from this complex embodied in the legal concepts . . . which make up the legal subculture' (1969: 66, original italics); and, as we have seen, this subculture may be more or it may be less present in empirical societies.

It is clear, however, that in many respects Fallers retains the analytic distinction between (in Smith's terms) the 'political' and 'administrative' and sees law as an expression of the latter. 'The varying authority of [the royal] governments, as manifested in their varying ability to compete with the A[frican] L[ocal] G[overnment] courts for jurisdiction over rights in land may be viewed as an index of the differentiation of rights in land from political authority—an index of the "legalisation", in the sense of rendering more subject to law, of a field of Soga life which was formerly governed to a greater degree by political considerations' (1969: 254). However, this opposition between law and politics, while clearly applicable to societies that institutionalise their decision-making processes along these separate lines, is not a universal analytic distinction that can be applied to those which do not; and Fallers makes it clear that judicial office in Busoga is indeed differentiated from other decision-making roles (1969: 331). At several points, Fallers's notion of law seems to identify it with what we have described as 'declaratory' law and to have little or no room for the 'executive' conception which suggests itself in Lesotho.

The answer to the problem lies, perhaps, in two factors: the nature of the judicial role, and the status of the legal norms invoked by the courts. As we saw in Chapter 1, it is not enough to distinguish between tribunals that operate with a superordinate judge and those that do not. The office of 'judge' can be filled in a variety of ways, which have implications for the kind of system that results. In the first place, disputes may be settled by reference to a person or set of persons who emerge as leaders or 'judges' by their personal attainments and influence, and who exercise their powers on an informal, non-institutional and largely arbitral basis. At the opposite end of the scale, matters may be referred to specialised, professional judges who have no other major social or political role, and who possess unique and compulsory jurisdiction by virtue of their office. But intermediate between the two there is the case of the Sotho chief, who indeed exercises 'judicial' authority by virtue of his office, and furthermore enjoys unique and compulsory jurisdiction, but who is neither professional nor specialised, having instead a variety of other functions to discharge which are neither institutionally nor conceptually differentiated from his work and role as 'judge'. For Fallers, this lack of differentiation is enough itself to shift the 'legal subculture' of the Basotho some way back towards the 'less legalistic' pole of the continuum: for Gulliver, the fact that there is a superordinate judge at all is enough to make the system ideally and essentially 'legal' as against 'political', the 'political' elements that survive being, as we have seen, somehow distortions or corruptions of his judicial role. Neither interpretation is adequate for the Sotho case. The distinctively normative quality which is the hallmark of law enters into those areas of chiefly decision-making that fall outside the 'judicial' or 'declaratory' category.

As we have seen, the norms of Sotho law are at once concrete and *general*. The formulae of the law consist of general principles rather than of progressively narrower and more specific deductions from them. Of course, when a dispute arises and a decision is reached, these general principles take specific form; but the law is particularised *in action*, and after the legal process is over, it reverts, so to speak, to its generality; future applications of the law start from that general level and not, as in a systematically deductive system, from the particular specification of the law in other decided cases. As we have seen, too, the norms of Sotho law can coexist in spite of their potential inconsistency, since it is only in concrete applications that this inconsistency becomes visible—and it is precisely this that enables the court or the chief to arrive at a conclusion which is at once a 'decision' and an act of the law. In a 'declaratory' system, where role differentiation is intense and the law a strictly professional field,[9] the issues between disputants are narrowly specified and the range of relevancy sharply circumscribed. Like cases (ideally, at least) lead to like outcomes, though as often as not the likeness is very largely a juristic artifact. In such a context, the more particular a decision or an emergent rule of law, the higher its juristic status tends to be; advocates argue on decided cases, rather than in terms of general principles, the range of whose application has been limited by previous case-law. The contrary is the case in Lesotho. Role-differentiation, though real enough along certain political dimensions (notably between chief and subject) is institutionally restricted along others. The small scale of the immediate legal community and the unitary character of the chiefly role mean that disputants join issue around a complex of enmeshed relationships, where rules of evidence and criteria of relevancy expand or contract to meet the perceived range of interaction between all persons involved. One case is not easily seen as 'on all fours' with another, since a core of 'relevant' likenesses cannot be readily extracted from the totality of events, relationships and issues in the dispute. In consequence, particular decisions carry little or no weight in subsequent cases; contrary to 'declaratory' practice, the more specific the legal expression of a norm, the more its juristic status is diminished. In the abstract, Sotho law is thus relatively unpredictable in its outcomes, and it is perhaps this feature that tempts the observer to see its operation in terms of politics or power. But the unpredictability does not stem from 'administrative discretion' so much as from the dense texture of the facts on which the decision is based. It is here that the norms of the law, by virtue of their very generality, enable lawful decisions to be arrived at which are no less legitimate for being unconstrained.[10]

Fallers suggests that the variations which empirical societies display in their 'legal subcultures' can be related to the institutional differentiation of the judicial office from the litigant public. Taking his hypothesis from Weber, he argues that 'functionally differentiated groups tend to develop distinctive subcultures and to pursue "interests" defined by these subcultures, all the while further elaborating and refining ("rationalising") them' (1969: 329), and he finds that the evidence of the four African societies which he considers supports this view. It would be a sterile and pedantic 'typologism' to try to pin-point the exact position of the Basotho in quite these terms on the continuum which Fallers proposes, especially since we have seen that some of his presuppositions do not square with the present line of argument. But the general reference to 'functionally differentiated groups' in relation to law and legal process can be followed up in terms of the internal operation of Sotho law itself, typological map-reading aside. A good case can be made for the view that Sotho law tends to be more specific at those points where functionally differentiated groups are brought into relationship, and less specific in areas where such differentiation is absent or less intense. (Though the line of thought pursued here is rather different from his, the correlation between normative specificity and functional differentiation would also fit Fallers's 'legalistic' analysis quite well.)

The reader will be able to discover his own instances in the text, but there are three that seem worth spelling out more explicitly by way of example. These concern (a) the legal relationship between the pastures and the arable lands (b) the laws relating to land allocation on the one hand and land deprivation on the other; and (c) what has not been encountered before, the rules of process that apply to bridewealth obligations.

(a) *Pastures and arable lands.* The general rule, that the soil belongs to the nation, applies in broad terms to all the earth-borne resources of the country, and thus to the pastures and the arable lands alike. But below this level of generality, certain distinctive discriminations begin to appear. There is, to start with, an ecologically derived differentiation between the two, arising out of the different uses to which land is put in the cattle-post country on the one hand and in the arable lowlands and foothills on the other. Moreover, in social terms, this differentiation sets up a relationship of 'organic' rather than 'mechanical' solidarity between the communities, the two ecological zones being enmeshed functionally in that the lowland stockowners send their cattle to the mountain pastures in the summer, whilst the mountain dwellers rely on the lowlands for many of their own essential supplies and foodstuffs. We have seen, in the chapter dealing with land-tenure, that —within the overall principle that applies to all land resources—the law and administration applying to the two categories of land display certain differences; the cattle-post country is subject to rules of the highest generality, whereas arable lands are controlled by rather more detailed and particular provisions.

(b) *Allocation and deprivation.* We have seen that the rules relating to the deprivation of land are more specific than those that concern its allocation. So far as the latter is concerned, the law does little more than enunciate certain rather general principles; in deprivation, however, it supplies more detailed and specific rules controlling the chief's powers and protecting the land-holder's tenure. It is not, perhaps, fanciful to see a relationship here between the specificity of the law and the functional differentiation of the parties involved. Where land is to be allocated, only two social positions are essentially to be distinguished: the chief who holds the vacant land on the one hand and the landless applicant on the other. (There may well be several applicants, of course, but these are functionally differentiated not from each other but only from the chief.) By contrast, where land is to be withdrawn, there are in principle three elements in the case: the chief, the landless applicants, and the existing land-holder himself.

(c) *Bridewealth obligations.* There are two important rules of Sotho law in regard to debt. One of them states that debts do not cancel each other out. This can be regarded as a strict and highly specific rule of procedure, implying as it does a concern to distinguish the capacities in which parties are appearing before the court, to impose restrictive and 'legalistic' tests of relevancy, and to segregate issues. The 'total relationship' between the parties seems to be subordinated here to a precise concern with the segregation of roles. The other rule states that debts do not prescribe (lapse with time). In contrast to the first, this could be regarded as a generous and non-legalistic rule, emphasising substantive rather than formal justice and ignoring technical 'legalisms' such as prescription or time bar. So far from being a specific type of rule, its main function is to make the legal process *less* specific and to align it more closely to the diffuse expectations of ordinary social life. Both these rules[11] find their commonest application in the field of bridewealth payments. On the one hand, affinal relationships would be exposed to uncertainty if any kind of communal accounting cancelled debts against each other and left only net credits and debits outstanding. A man might find himself owing three head of cattle to a family with whom he had no affinal relationship recognisable to him at all. The rule against set-off ensures that bridewealth reciprocities are not cancelled out in this way and that affinal relationships are concretely and individually structured along identifiable and specific transfers of cattle. Each debt is a separate obligation that must be specifically rendered. Conversely, the rule that debts do not prescribe is a necessary one, given that on the basis of an ideal standard payment of twenty cattle relatively few households could afford to pay all of them at once. The debt must be allowed to carry over into the next generation if necessary, and in fact cases involving bridewealth debts occur that involve obligations going back over thirty years and more.

Thus, a rule that has a highly specific character is associated with the structural differentiation between exchanging affinal groups, whilst a rule of a general and 'non-legalistic' kind is associated with dimensions of structure that emphasise the homogeneity and continuity of the lineage enduring through time. The difference between the rules can, of course, be explained concretely by relating them, as we have seen, to the functional necessities of marriage alliance as an empirical institution. But the concept of differentiation is not introduced as a rival but rather as a supplementary means of analysis. It suggests how social structure and the nature of legal rules can be related to each other in a way that goes beyond statistical correlation on the one hand and mechanical causality on the other. It is not simply that one kind of rule is 'found to occur' in association with one kind of structure or relationship, nor that when a given rule is explained in terms of the functional necessities of a particular institution analysis must then stop. The rule and the institution alike are open to an explanatory account that includes them both within the wider notion of differentiation.

In conclusion, let us return to the central preoccupations of the argument in this book, re-asserting the essential features of the kind of law it has examined and placing them squarely against the interpretation it rejects. The judicial/administrative polarity—like that of authority/power, which it mirrors—suggests a framework in which each of the two terms has certain attributes and an ideal sphere of operation. Thus, the *judicial* is seen as rule-governed, and hence constrained, and is concerned with the area of right; the *administrative* is seen as discretionary, and hence free, and is concerned with the area of power. But these oppositions do not enter into that 'executive law' which was described in Chapter 1 as the characteristic legality of chieftainship, and of which customary law is perhaps not so much a synonym as a special case.[12] It has already been suggested that to follow a rule is not necessarily to be constrained; and it is a feature of Sotho law that an outcome can be both lawful and legitimate even though an alternative conclusion could be argued to be equally derivable from the 'rule', or from the coincidence of several —possibly inconsistent—'rules'.

It must be reiterated that what is involved here is not the familiar 'judicial' criterion of whether or not the act in question fell within the *competence* of the actor. According to this criterion, an outcome is lawful if it falls within the area of 'discretion' left 'free' by circumambient rules—if the chief, in other words, is acting 'within his authority' in the exercise of his power.[13] The proposition advanced here is not of this kind. It is certainly the case that a Sotho chief must keep within the circumscription of his particular office and authority; but it is not the case that all his acts within that circumscribed area are surrendered to a 'discretion' fettered only by the rules of judicial review. Legality enters into his decisions as well as bounding them, and these are in principle open to challenge on their merits. Conversely, it is not the case that legality itself is constrained by 'decision-inevitability' in such a way as to imply a unique outcome. The 'rules' of customary law reside in concrete but general norms, whose ambivalence, or ambiguity, permits a variety of possible outcomes, each one of which can be formally proposed and argued for as 'legitimate'. It is true that one face of this is that what are in effect 'political' outcomes receive a factitious and *post factum* legitimation derived from norms that would justify almost any decision. This is the point at which the ambivalence in all *Herrschaft* is found, and it is here that the current dilemma of chieftainship has become explicit: the folk-ways, and the ways of the folk in power. But a facile reductionism only obscures the contours of *all* legitimacy, obliterating the discontinuities of consciousness and offering in their place a *platteland* of undifferentiated 'interests' that falsify the empirical reality while purporting to explain it.

This is the tendency of both Marxist and positivist 'social control' conceptions of the normative universe of action. Marxism, at least in its more sophisticated forms, has the merit of acknowledging the reality of legitimacy, while characterising it (often very convincingly) as 'false consciousness'; the theoretical difficulty here is that it is not easy to see what criterion of falseness can itself escape the toils of 'consciousness' in the end: and if none can, then what it is that enables the judgment to be made. Malinowskian positivism, on the other hand, simply fails to take seriously the specificity of law itself, since it has no means of handling the problem of consciousness at all. Durkheim (1912) confronted the same issues in his study of religion, and although his solution is certainly highly vulnerable, it offers insights into an anthropology or sociology of law that deserve exploration. Much of *Elementary Forms of the Religious Life* could be reformulated as an analysis of law in society, with the 'normative' replacing the 'sacred' as the organising concept. The substitution of 'mediations' for 'interdictions' (taboos) would provide a conceptual bridge between orders of reality which are related in a way that Durkheim was aware of but which, in his anxiety to underline the *dichotomies* of religious action, he never adequately explained. But the issue is, as he recognised, one of linkages between discrete orders of social reality, not points along a continuum. Social control doctrines, whether of a positivist or vulgar-Marxist kind, fall short of the reality of law, just as the doctrines of his contemporaries fell short, in Durkheim's eyes, of the reality of religion. For the other face of executive law is to acknowledge no power that is not also legitimate authority, to reject the dichotomy of 'right' on the one hand and discretion or freedom on the other, and to bring into conjunction the divided and distinguished worlds which the folklore of 'judiciality' sets apart.

Not the least interesting aspect of these processes is that the deceptions and 'false consciousness' of executive law—its temptation to obscure the bifurcation and intertwining of legitimacy and self-interest—should be so neatly paralleled by the equal inability of judicial systems to conform to the requirements of their own ideal theory. The presence of an institutionally specific legislature—the precondition of any plausible judicial system—cannot eliminate the need for decision, nor can it, at the level of theory, constrain or determine the decision that is made. In practice, however, it can obscure the nature of the decision-making process that is involved, by presenting the outcome as *inevitable*, and thus as not a 'decision' at all; conversely, what is not inevitable is not seen as law. But to give a reason is not to postulate an efficient cause, nor is it to argue for a logically unique outcome; the juristic repertoire at the disposal of Sotho customary law enables a decision to be both reasonable and legitimate, since norms are not progressively specified into constraining rules, and can therefore remain reasonable, while decision-making is normatively controlled, and can therefore remain legitimate.

Appendix 1   Case study: the chieftainship dispute at Patlong[1]

This is an account and analysis of the long and hotly contested dispute over the chieftainship of Patlong.[2] It illustrates many of the main issues discussed in the text relating to succession, inheritance, marriage, the seniority of houses, the 'family council', the placing system and the political anthropology of chieftainship. No less importantly, it yields great insight into the general character of Sotho litigation—the argumentation adopted, the style of legal debate, and the attitudes of litigants, witnesses and judges to the law as a whole.

Patlong is an important chieftainship on the Orange River within the Principal Ward of Qacha's Nek, located near the village of Sekake's (see the map on page 4, 28.4 E. 30.1 3). It is ruled by the senior segment of the Mosothoane maximal lineage, whose principal segments are shown on figures 11 and 12.

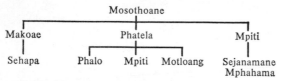

FIGURE 11   *The sons of Mosothoane*

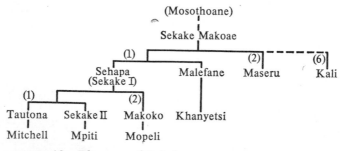

FIGURE 12   *The sons of Sekake*

116

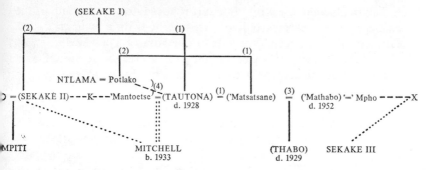

FIGURE 13   Sekake *v*. Tautona

Key

Brackets (THABO) mean that the person named had died before the major hearing.

A broken line – – – – – – – indicates sexual relation outside marriage. With the letter 'K'– – – –K– – – –it indicates a *kenelo* (leviratic) union.

A dotted line. . . . . .shows physical paternity. Double dots : : : : : indicate *kenelo* birth.

The figures in brackets (1) (2) indicate order of seniority between siblings or wives as the case may be.

The symbol '=' (*viz.*, in quotation marks) denotes woman-marriage.

Sehapa Sekake (usually referred to as Sekake I in this narrative) had two sons in his first house, Tautona (the elder) and Sekake II (see figure 13). Tautona succeeded his father on the latter's death and ruled until he himself died in 1928. His marriages constitute one of the most contentious items in the dispute, but at this point in the exposition we may regard him as having had five wives, in the following order of seniority: (i) 'Matsatsane (Lefa) (ii) Likotoeng (iii) 'Mathabo (iv) 'Mantoetse (v) 'Masebueng. (Figure 13 omits those that do not figure further in the case.)

At Tautona's death in 1928, there was no male issue in the first or second house. In the third house, there was an infant son, Thabo, who died shortly afterwards in 1929. The fourth and fifth houses were also barren of issue in 1928. However, in 1933, 'Mantoetse in the fourth house became the mother of Mitchell, the child of a leviratic union (*kenelo*) between herself and her late husband's younger brother Sekake II. Sekake, who had also acted as regent for the young child Thabo in the short interval between Tautona's death and the boy's, had a son by his own marriage. This was Mpiti, who raised the action here discussed.

Tautona's marriage in his fourth house forms an important element in the case. He lived irregularly with a woman called Potlako, who was herself the wife of one Ntlama Tlhakanelo. It was alleged that Tautona married 'Mantoetse into the same 'house', as a *ngoetsi* or subsidiary wife to Potlako, apparently at the latter's insistence.

In 1935, the chieftainship of Patlong passed to 'Mathabo, Tautona's third wife, and she reigned in her own right until her execution in 1952. However, during the course of her long reign she attempted to raise an heir to the chieftainship in her own house by entering into a woman-marriage with Mpho, who in due course gave birth to a child, Sekake III, whom 'Mathabo sought to have recognised as successor. (An alternative view is that 'Mathabo married Mpho to the grave of her dead son Thabo.) 'Mathabo's action, which she justified on the grounds that, as full chieftainess, she 'was Tautona' and 'ate' all his rights, was accepted by some of the Sons of Makoae but opposed by others.

There thus emerged three possible claimants to the chieftainship of Patlong: Mpiti, Mitchell and Sekake III. The dispute, however, is dominated by the first two of these.

The first record is of a dispute between Sekake II and chieftainess 'Mathabo in 1941. It appears from the judgment of the Civil Appeal Court that Sekake had been convicted and fined by the Paramount Chief for an assault on 'Mathabo. This was provoked, according to Sekake, by her dalliance with an outsider, one Rahlolo, which Sekake regarded as an affront to his position as male head of the family with *kenelo* (leviratic) rights over her. At the time, Sekake II was also 'Mathabo's principal counsellor. The conviction was upheld.

In October 1949, 'Mathabo attempted some form of *coup* on behalf of her 'son' Sekake III. 'Mantoetse rallied the sons of Makoae into opposing this move, whereupon 'Mathabo took the matter to the Chief's court. At some point in the early 1950s, the dispute came before the (administrative) court of the Principal Chief of Qacha's Nek. From the judgment of this court, it appears that 'Mathabo named her sons in order of succession as Sekake III, then Mitchell, then Mitchell's two younger brothers in the house of 'Mantoetse. She thus assumed all the children of Tautona as her sons (she being chieftainess) and ranked them in order of seniority. Against her, it was argued that the custom of woman-marriage was illegal; and that even if it were not, Mpho would be no more than an insignificant wife, a *lefielo* or 'broom', in the house of Makoae, whose son could not be successor to the chieftainship. The men of the court at Qacha's Nek rejected 'Mathabo's claim, arguing somewhat inconsistently that there was insufficient evidence of woman-marriage for it to be accepted as legitimate custom, and also that such marriages had been a source of incessant unrest in the nation. (It may be that the second part of this argument related to 'secondary' marriages in general, while the first referred more specifically to woman-marriage.) Mitchell was accepted as the son of 'Mantoetse, whose possible status as a junior wife to Potlako was not, at this stage, brought in as an issue.

The records then show that in 1952, following 'Mathabo's death, the Principal Chief called upon the 'family' in its wide sense—the sons of Mosothoane—to propose a successor. In November of that year, Patlong ward reported back to the chief that 'the family gives you Mpiti Sekake as the guardian of Mitchell Tautona', adding that 'a group of the people, being men of Patlong, gives you Mpiti Sekake to be chief, not guardian'. Thirty-nine voices were raised for the first of these motions, and thirty-six for the second; however, it was stressed that 'we do not consider the number of votes, but we of the family wish to inform you that there have been different opinions', and the Chief was invited to convene a further meeting in Patlong if he wished to hear for himself.

Within a week or so, the chief sent three representatives to Patlong, who were present at a meeting of the sons of Mosothoane and of the people of Patlong. The chairman was Kali Sekake, a junior son in Sekake's house, who had been appointed as acting chief after 'Mathabo's arrest. Mpho, 'Mantoetse and Mpiti were among those who spoke. Mpho seems simply to have declared her position as having been married into 'Mathabo's house and having borne an heir to the chieftainship in the person of Sekake III. 'Mantoetse argued for Mitchell, as heir to the second house, there being no male issue in the first. Mpiti, for tactical reasons that the record does not disclose, appears to have acknowledged Mitchell as heir, with himself as the second in line. Some difference expressed itself between the sons of Makoae, or a large group of them, who favoured Mitchell, and a wider section of the people of Patlong, supported by a smaller Makoae faction, in favour of Mpiti. The Principal Chief seems to have favoured Mitchell, or at least discountenanced Mpiti. The

upshot was (at least according to Kali's report) that the sons of Mosothoane agreed on Mitchell as successor, with Mpiti as regent until
the boy reached his majority. They went on to propose Mpiti as the
successor of his own father to the chieftainship of Thabana-
Ts'ooana, a major headmanship within the ward of Patlong. The
Principal Chief's representatives reported this proposition back, while
acknowledging that it was not part of their original brief. For the rest,
at all events, it is clear that the Principal Chief accepted the report and
acknowledged Mitchell as heir, with Mpiti as regent and guardian.

However, this outcome failed to satisfy either 'Mantoetse, who did
not welcome Mpiti as guardian to her son, or Mpiti himself, who now
reasserted (if indeed he had ever really withdrawn) his claim to the
full chieftainship. Mpiti declined to appear before his Principal
Chief for confirmation in any junior capacity, and in July 1953 made
an open bid for control by assuming the chieftainship of Patlong.
The dispute that this action sparked off came before the Paramount
Chief in January 1955, and the case was heard on her behalf by two
senior chiefs (one of them the chief of Majara's, successor to Moshoeshoe I's fourth cardinal linc).

The Paramount Chief's Court

A major preoccupation of the court was the fact, admitted on all
sides, that 'Mathabo had been appointed as chieftainess in her own
right, not as regent, and that she continued in this position until
her death. Mpiti argued that this was an implicit denial of Mitchell's
claim, since if there were in fact a direct male heir to the late chief,
which Mitchell held himself out to be, then 'Mathabo would only
have been a regent for that heir, since women become full chiefs only
if there is no male son.[3] Accordingly, in the absence of such an heir
(as implied by 'Mathabo's status as full chief), the proviso in the
Laws of Lerotholi (1946) section 2 applied, in terms of which 'if a
chief dies leaving no male issue, the chieftainship shall devolve upon
the male following according to the succession of houses'. According to Mpiti, this would have brought the succession to his own
father, Sekake II, and thence to him.

The Paramount Chief's court countered this initiative of Mpiti's
by pointing out that 'Mathabo's proclamation as a chieftainess in
her own right actually negated Mpiti's argument, since Tautona's
chieftainship had not in fact passed to Sekake II. Moreover, the

Laws of Lerotholi were silent on questions of posthumous children,[4] and therefore did not exclude the succession from passing to them. The court went further, and opined that even if Mpiti were right in his theory of fraternal succession, this was a custom that was falling into desuetude and no longer a determinant factor in the issue. The published *Laws of Lerotholi* were described as 'a mere declaration of custom, rather than laws' which, as such, could be overtaken by change. The judges then rather abruptly switched direction, and asserted that the law of posthumous succession held good, no matter what any declaration might purport to lay down. No doubt the judges were embarrassed by the fact that Paramount Chief Griffith's succession in 1913 was a case both of fraternal succession and of the rejection of posthumously conceived issue. The decision was, accordingly, unequivocally for Mitchell, Mpiti being stripped even of his position as regent and guardian and 'Mantoetse appointed in his place.

But before Mitchell's confirmation and Mpiti's rejection were confirmed, the Resident Commissioner and the Paramount Chief agreed to allow Mpiti an opportunity to test his claim once more in the courts, Mitchell's nomination continuing to be accepted for administrative purposes meanwhile, but without prejudice to Mpiti's eventual rights. The case was obviously one concerning customary law, and a special court was set up to hear it, under the experienced president A. D. Maime. The hearing took place at Qacha's Nek in November and December 1957.

The special court

After a fairly uncontroversial rehearsal of some basic facts, Mpiti presented his case by arguing that Mitchell was not lawfully born to 'Mantoetse in such a way as to entitle him to succeed to the chieftainship. He was in law the child of Potlako, and Ntlama Tlhakanelo's son by cattle. He elaborated this assertion by explaining the 'Mantoetse had been married with cattle taken as fines from men who had committed adultery with Potlako; the latter being, of course, the wife of Ntlama, it was to him that the cattle belonged. (This became one of the central grounds of Mpiti's case and was argued this way and that throughout the proceedings.) Mpiti also relied on what he alleged to be the defects inherent in a leviratic birth, but his more radical attack was designed to challenge the lawfulness of 'Mantoetse's marriage to Tautona, and thus deny Mitchell's legitimacy root and branch. If 'Mantoetse had been married for Potlako, she could have no greater marital status than the latter, who was no wife at all. The irregularities in Tautona's use of cattle were brought in as still further proof that the marriage was void.

But before leading evidence on the facts, Mpiti introduced Chief Goliath Moshoeshoe as his first witness.[5] Goliath appeared as an expert witness, to speak to the law, and denied any knowledge of the particular facts under dispute. This was, in fact, somewhat disingenuous, since it was known, and emerged before the court, that Mpho (the genetrix of Sekake III) was a daughter of Goliath's junior brother Jagersfontein. Much of the earlier part of Goliath's evidence was taken up by a display of legal and historical virtuosity, and backed his claim to expert knowledge and long experience in the adjudication of questions of succession. On the issue of *kenelo* (the levirate), he stated that posthumous children were incorporated into the family of the woman to whom they were born, since a child is begotten by cattle—'belched by a beast'. However, when a woman is seduced, if the husband sues the seducer and receives a fine of cattle, the child born to the woman cannot be heir, although he is legitimated. Alternatively, the bridewealth can be returned and the wife dismissed, in which case she takes the child with her and belongs to his mother's people. Goliath also seems to have expressed the view (in the light of subsequent comment from witnesses and from the court) that a posthumous child can be heir to an inheritance (*lefa*) but not successor to a chieftainship. It is, however, not clear whether he was really intending to express this view or rather to draw a distinction between the issue of a true leviratic union and the child of a less regular liaison.

He went on to say that when a chief takes cattle that have been allocated to a particular house in order to get himself another wife, the woman so acquired is the wife of that house; but that if he takes them from the unallocated portion of the herd, then he can place the new wife in any house, or establish her in one of her own. Goliath, professing to take the facts as he was told them, gave it as his opinion that the cattle for 'Mantoetse had been taken from Potlako's kraal, and that she had therefore been married to Potlako's 'house'; but since Potlako was not the true wife of a house, 'Mantoetse was no wife either, Mitchell was not the true son of the levirate, and the succession passed through Sekake II to Mpiti.

The rest of Mpiti's witnesses testified to the facts of the case. Mokhele Chitja, a self-confessed but plausible thief, agreed that 'Mantoetse had been married to Potlako, and that the cattle paid for her were those of Potlako's kraal, including those that had been taken as fines for her adulteries. Potlako was not married to Tautona; and in fact when Tautona himself had been fined at Ntlama's behest for his own adultery with her, she had pretended to go home to her husband with the fines, but had instead absconded and returned to Tautona, bringing the cattle with her. (Chitja explained that he did not mean 'cattle with hooves'; there were, in fact, four horses and £40 in cash, but he adopted the common Sotho convention of referring to all payments in certain kinds of transaction as 'cattle'.)

'Malefa, the next witness, was another woman who had been married into Potlako's establishment, and she confirmed that it was Potlako who had chosen 'Mantoetse, although Tautona had wanted to take another woman. 'Masebueng, the last of Tautona's wives, had little of interest to say.

She was followed by Mpho, who testified that 'Mathabo had taken her 'as a womb' for the third house, to raise up an heir to the chieftainship; she claimed that the sons of Sekake had deprived her house of its rights. Like several witnesses, Mpho put up an unconvincing pretence of ignorance, even going so far as to claim that it was only on the day the case opened in court that she was aware that a dispute over the chieftainship was in progress. Admittedly she had no reason to love either Mpiti or Mitchell, but her protestations of ignorance and impartiality were clearly largely due to her anxiety not to prejudice her own position for the future by alienating either of her potential chiefs.

Bolepeletsa, who followed, was not so much a supporter of Mpiti as an adviser and confidant of the late 'Mathabo, and was called as a witness because of his opposition to Mitchell. His view, however, was that Mitchell was the heir and successor in his own house, but that the chieftainship could not pass to him. He thus took up a less radical position than those who denied Mitchell's filiation altogether.

Chief Phalo Phatela, senior headman at Sekitsing in the adjoining Principal Chiefdom of Phamong, and a son of Mosothoane like the others, testified that Tautona had taken adultery fines for Potlako and used them to marry 'Mantoetse into Potlako's house. 'Mantoetse was thus never a wife. He also maintained that the custom of the levirate was falling into disuse, though he did not draw any distinction between inheritance and succession, and did not consider the argument that the relevant date for the alleged desuetude of *kenelo* was not 1957, but 1933, the year of Mitchell's birth.

Mitchell Tautona then opened his case on the other side. Most of his own evidence followed a predictable pattern. He affirmed that as Tautona's son by the levirate he was successor of Patlong, and that Mpiti had at first accepted this. He maintained that he had been installed as chief shortly after 'Mathabo's death in 1952, and denied that he had been either under 'Mantoetse's guardianship or installed as an acting chief.

He called 'Mantoetse as his first witness. The essential part of her testimony related, of course, to her own marriage. She pointed out that Mpiti's father Sekake II had lived with her leviratically after Tautona's death, thus impliedly acknowledging the validity of her marriage. And she claimed that 'Mathabo, as chieftainess, had never objected to this. Mpiti, she said, had without protest even used 'Mathabo's cattle in 'Mantoetse's house, which he would never have done had he declined to recognise her as Tautona's widow. But she admitted that Potlako was not Tautona's wife, though she went on to claim that she herself had never been a part of Potlako's establishment. She had been brought up as a wife by 'Matsatsane (of the first house), and misunderstandings could have arisen from the fact that Potlako had also at one time had a sleeping hut in the same enclosure. Her, 'Mantoetse's, own marriage was a lawful marriage by cattle and was independent of Potlako, and her son Mitchell was the lawful chief.

Mitchell's mother was followed by Kali Sekake Makoae, of a junior house in Sekake's lineage and senior headman at Maboloka within the ward of Patlong; he had acted as chief during 'Mathabo's trial and been chairman of the meeting held in 1952 to discuss the succession issue. It was Kali who now testified that Mpho was brother's daughter to Goliath. He stated that the family had objected to 'Mathabo's arrangement with Mpho, not so much on general principles concerning woman-marriage as because Tautona's wife 'Mantoetse had borne her son Mitchell, thus making it unnecessary to resort to special means to raise up a successor. He went on to speak about Mpiti's private life and conduct, bringing into the open certain matters that had only been hinted at before, all more or less to Mpiti's discredit. Mpiti had, in fact, been convicted on several occasions of fairly slight offences. He was also disapproved of for living at a beer-hall and for having married a Griqua wife. In Kali's view, these delinquencies virtually disqualified him from succeeding to the chieftainship.

Kali was quite ready to agree that Potlako was not a wife of Tautona, but of Ntlama. 'Mantoetse's marriage to Tautona however was not affected by anything that Potlako did or was. Whore, thief and self-seeker, she was regretted by no one (though Mpiti's failure to call her as a witness was held against him when the court came to consider its judgment).

The Principal Chief of Qacha's Nek, Theko Makhaola, came next. He confined himself largely to formal evidence, and while affirming the fact of Mitchell's appointment, showed every sign of standing aloof from the dispute, 'I have tried my best to get to the root of this trouble, but without success.' (It emerged however that Mitchell's wife was a daughter of Theko's junior brother Makhaola.)

The next witness was Molaoli Sekake, a subject and kinsman of Kali's at Maboloka. He added little of substance to what had gone before, but was called as a member of the house of Makoae who had been present at the critical meetings of the sons of Mosothoane and could speak to what had taken place there. Sekake Posholi followed, as a son of Sekake, and confirmed that 'Mathabo's attempt to promote Sekake III (Mpho's son) had been rejected by the family. He averred that 'Mantoetse was Tautona's wife and denied that the cattle taken out for her had belonged to Potlako.

The headman of Kolo-la-Ts'oene, Mocketi Mapheelle, followed and introduced some new factors. According to him—and he claimed close acquaintance with Tautona—'Mantoetse's father Rantebale had not only demanded the high bridewealth of twenty-three beasts for his daughter, but had asked to have them all at once. He also stated that it had been Tautona's first wife, 'Matsatsane, who had asked her husband to look after Potlako (her younger sister), since she was unhappy with Ntlama. The cattle paid as fines for Potlako were used by Tautona to provide bridewealth for junior sons of Sekake, instead of being kept as chieftainship beasts and kraaled at 'Mathabo's where the chieftainess could have used their milk and dung. He went on to deny that 'Mathabo had any original right to the chieftainship (he had been engaged in a dispute with her over Kolo-la-Ts'oene) and advanced the interesting proposition that a man who consorted with a concubine was entitled to the adultery fines taken on her behalf, if the woman's husband did not claim them. (There is some ambiguity in this. One view—the older one— is that fines are kept by the chief, who will usually pass a proportion on to the wronged man. The more modern view is that they are in fact damages, and go to the injured person direct. Moeketi's evidence seems to argue in both senses and to be consistent with neither.) He, too, agreed that Potlako was not Tautona's wife.

Motloang Phatela's evidence added little, unless the record is correct in attributing to him the statement that Mitchell was a son of 'Mathabo, since he was the child of her late husband Tautona. This probably was his argument, since he went on to discuss (though without answering) the question of whether 'Mathabo had speci- fically sought a leviratic union for 'Mantoetse. This opened a new road for Mitchell: suggesting that he could claim as successor to the late chieftainess as well as to Tautona himself. However, Motloang hedged his bets by asserting ignorance of whether Mitchell had been born before or after Tautona's death. His testimony was followed by a remarkable display of know-nothingism by Sejanamane, a major headman at Mphahama's. His repudiation of any knowledge of anything at all culminated in the memorable assertion that 'I have no knowledge of Sotho law and custom'. One of his problems was that he was clearly in great awe of his chief, 'Mantsebo Seisa; she was the widow of his elder brother, and Sejanamane did not like to suggest anything that might in any way be taken as a challenge to her rights; but the temptation seems to have been present in his mind.

The evidence of Sera Faso, a junior son of Mosothoane under Phatela, underlined the point that 'Mathabo's seed-raising by Mpho was superfluous since an heir already existed in the person of Mitchell, whom she could have adopted; and in other respects he supported the previous witnesses for the defendant.

Mitchell's last witness was Mopeli Makoko, headman of Qhoa- linyane in the ward of Patlong, and heir to Sekake's second house. He was one of the signatories to the letter sent to the Principal Chief in November 1952 reporting that the 'family' favoured Mitchell; Chief Phalo Phatela, Mpiti's witness, had also signed the letter, but later alleged that he had been coerced into doing so by Mopeli. Mopeli firmly repeated what had been said before, stressing the rejection of Sekake III and underlining that the great bulk of the sons of Mosothoane had given their support to Mitchell. Mopeli also stressed that 'Mathabo was not entitled to take any decisions on her own, and that her purported marriage to Mpho was unacceptable because she had acted without, or against, the authority of the sons of Sekake. On the issue between Mitchell and Mpiti, however, Mopeli alone of all the defendant's witnesses betrayed the fact that, after Mitchell's appointment, the 'people of Patlong' began to regret their choice and turned towards the plaintiff, Mpiti.

This concluded the evidence. The court produced a lengthy judgment, finding in favour of Mitchell and wholly rejecting Mpiti's claim. The judgment opened with a full rehearsal of the facts, and of the evidence put in by both sides. It was accepted as common cause that Potlako was never Tautona's wife, and it was stressed that the sons of Makoae had rejected 'Mathabo's claim for her son Sekake III. The court gave rather sceptical attention to Goliath's evidence, and recalled his relationship to Mpho. It rejected what it read as his contention that a posthumously conceived son had no rights of succession while still retaining rights of inheritance. Having had the advantage of actually hearing Goliath, the court may well be correct in its reading, though, as has been noted, the record could rather more easily be read as stating that in Goliath's view there was a crucial difference between the child of levirate and less regular issue. But it certainly seems probable that Goliath, while wishing to keep his foot in the door of high rank in Lesotho, was reluctant to say anything that might be interpreted as a challenge to the throne.

Mpiti's argument that 'Mantoetse could not have been Tautona's wife since she was married for Potlako was neatly turned on its head when the court read 'Mantoetse's testimony as indicating that precisely because Potlako was not the wife of Tautona, she ('Mantoetse) could not have been married for her. This was therefore the second time that Mpiti had been hoist on his own petard.

The main legal argument that confronted the court was that based upon the proviso to the *Laws of Lerotholi* (1946) section 2, which, as we have seen, stated that 'if a chief dies leaving no male issue the chieftainship shall devolve upon the male following according to the succession of houses'. But, as in the Paramount Chief's Court, the line of thought adopted was that nothing in the law stipulated that a posthumously conceived child could not assume his father's rights and duties. The words 'dies without leaving male issue' were thus explicitly interpreted to exclude the case of *kenelo* (levirate). The court went on to repeat its rejection of Goliath's evidence on law, and affirmed that 'the law does not divide a man's rights into two parts; in declaring him an heir, it makes him an integral successor'. This was in fact somewhat to distort as well as to overstate the point. Mpiti was not, of course, arguing that Mitchell could be chief but must lose the inheritance; he was arguing that whatever happened to the inheritance Mitchell could not be chief. Moreover, the law does recognise that chieftainship rights and property rights are separable; for example, a deposed chief does not lose any of his estate; and there had already been evidence in the case, and from the defendant's witnesses, that Tautona's chieftainship fields had been differently disposed from his own personal allocation during 'Mathabo's reign. But the court's point was nevertheless well taken, in that if Mitchell was Tautona's son by cattle he was also his son in respect of chieftainship. Since, then, it accepted 'Mantoetse's marriage and Mitchell's legitimate if leviratic birth, it followed that it rejected Mpiti's claim *in toto*.

Six months later Mpiti formally lodged an appeal to the Judicial Commissioner. His basic argument still rested on the *Laws of Lerotholi*, but he added some further and often subtle (if highly debatable) points as well. He argued that by the time Mitchell was born, Thabo was long dead, so that Sekake II (Mpiti's father) was no longer regent to the then heir and could not pass on rights to 'Mantoetse's child. Thabo's premature death also explained why regency was not an issue between 'Mathabo and Sekake II: the chieftainess's reign did not interrupt the succession. Mpiti was right about this, whatever may be said of the implications he deduced from it. A chieftainess in her own right reigns till her death, when the succession resumes its normal line. The real issue is one of 'vesting'. If the right vests unconditionally *a morte* of the (male) chief, then Sekake II passed on his right to Mpiti. If it is simply conditional vesting, then the successor is looked for *a morte* of the chieftainess, so that other things being equal Mitchell would succeed (of course, Mpiti had the auxiliary claim that other things were not equal, since Mitchell was no son of Tautona, but that is another point). The third possibility is that of vesting subject to defeasance, *viz.*, under a resolutive condition:[6] the succession vested in Sekake II but passed away from him again on Mitchell's (presumed legitimate) birth. But Mpiti's strength lay in the fact that an *installed* chief cannot lose his chieftainship by the subsequent birth of even a lawful son, and since 'Mathabo's reign does not interrupt the succession, the same right inheres in the male line to which the succession will eventually pass on her death. This argument was countered by asserting that the actual installation of a chief brings a new factor into the situation; a chief cannot lose his right to another after he has once been installed, but this does not apply to the case where he has not.

Mpiti was bold enough to bring out into the open the question of the Paramountcy, arguing that he was seeking to follow the law that gave Griffith the succession to Letsie II.[7] He went on to defend the view that one child could succeed to the estate and another to the chieftainship, arguing that in the absence of male issue the proviso to section two passed the succession to the junior house, though a posthumous child in a senior house could still inherit the personal estate of the deceased in that house. Finally, he returned to the point that had figured so strongly in the hearing, that the cattle taken out to marry 'Mantoetse were the fruit of fines taken out for Potlako's adultery, and thus invalidated the marriage.

The Judicial Commissioner's judgment can be very briefly considered. On 18 May 1959, Mr W. G. S. Driver upheld the Special Court, mainly on the grounds that 'even though the *kenelo* custom may be a decadent custom, it is still practised occasionally', and that Mitchell should therefore succeed.

At this point, the record stops, though Mpiti did not abandon his case, and prepared an appeal to the High Court and no doubt eventually beyond. Shortly after the Judicial Commissioner's hearing, Mpiti was returned as a member of the Legislative Council for Qacha's Nek. Under the 1959 Constitution, elections to this body were indirect, being made by the District Councils, these latter being elected by adult male suffrage; nevertheless, this circumstance goes some way to validate Mpiti's claim to popular support. He was elected as a representative of the Congress Party (BCP), the most radical of the political parties in the territory. He subsequently broke away from the Congress in what he claimed to me to be a 'leftward' direction; but this interpretation must be read in the light of the tortuous politics of African nationalist movements at the time and neither adds to nor detracts from the plausibility of his claim to popular backing in Patlong.

This completes the historical narrative; but there are several features of the case that will repay rather more analytical discussion. The account itself has probably revealed the sophistication of legal debate, especially evident on the two occasions when the court engaged in some juristic fencing with Mpiti that is wholly typical of Sotho skill in argument. These passages of arms also reveal a delicate awareness of the two 'moments' of legal argument—the enunciation of the law itself, and the determination of what this means for the particular decision in hand. Some constructive and fruitful ambiguities are exploited here. Thus, if Potlako is agreed not to have been married to Tautona, could 'Mantoetse have been married as a junior wife in Potlako's house? Obviously not, claims Mpiti: and argues that Mitchell is therefore not Tautona's son. Obviously not, agrees 'Mantoetse: from which the court concludes that she was not married for Potlako but was a wife in her own right. The question of the cattle (not necessarily, it will be remembered, 'cattle with hooves'), which formed a very important part of Mpiti's case, clearly revealed —and the point was not really disputed—that Tautona had behaved both immorally and illegally, not only in robbing Ntlama of his wife, but also in depriving him of his damages, on one occasion probably in conscious collusion with Potlako. But the court was able to sidestep this issue, since it was never clearly ascertained whether Tautona was simply at fault in not compensating Ntlama (and here the moot point arises of whether the cattle were damages or fines) or whether the cattle were not his at all. Where the 'cattle without hooves' take the form of cash, the ambivalence is profound enough to make it possible to evade a direct answer. It appears, indeed, from both positive and negative evidence not to be the case that bridewealth depends on the actual identity of particular beasts, still less of course on that of particular pound notes, though this question of identity may be evidentially important as a way of ascertaining who it was that paid the 'cattle' and from which house they were taken.[8]

One feature of the case that calls for rather fuller comment concerns the role and composition of the 'family council'. The account of succession and inheritance in Chapter 3 has shown that the most important element in the procedures following a death is the family's decision. The 'substantive rules' in the *Laws of Lerotholi* and elsewhere do not constitute an 'objective' law to which recourse is had if a 'private arrangement' cannot be agreed on, so much as a set of customary principles which reflect and also inform the council's deliberations. Three different elements can be analysed in this. First of all, there is the question of the law applicable to the matter; a case in point concerns the validity of woman-marriage. Second, there is the question of fact, which consists in identifying the person of the heir; in most cases, though certainly not in all, this is a straightforward matter, but it is nevertheless up to the family to decide, and to present the heir and successor of the deceased. Third, there is a question which would not, in Western-type courts, be considered a relevant issue at all, namely, whom it is that the family wish to advance or reject. These are, of course, analytical aspects, and in the actual decision it may be impossible to disentangle them. It is quite clear, for instance, that the greater part of the lineage were opposed to 'Mathabo's attempted *coup* on behalf of Sekake III, but they objected rather on the grounds that there was already an available heir in the person of Mitchell (whom she could have adopted into her house) than because the form of marriage between herself and the woman Mpho was illegal. It is also quite clear that many in the family were hostile to Mpiti and produced reasons for considering him to be an unsuitable person to have as chief. However, if the family had considered Mpiti to be a worthy candidate for the chieftainship, there was sufficient ambiguity in the law to have enabled them to make the opposite choice, and to do so in a manner that legitimated their decision in legal terms; this does not mean simply that they had a 'discretion' in the matter (making their decision an 'act in the law') but rather that they could assert a direct legal authority for the specific choice they made (an 'act of the law': Salmond 1947: 347).

Nevertheless, the degree and nature of the support for each candidate is in itself a matter of great importance, and there is, fortunately, enough evidence in the case to enable some facts to be retrieved. Four levels of lineage depth emerge, defined by reference to Sehapa, Sekake, Makoae and Mosothoane (Sehapa is the person shown as Sekake I in figures 11–13). The most important levels were the second—the sons of Sekake—and the fourth—the sons of Mosothoane. Mosothoane generated three houses, those of Makoae (the first house), Phatela and Mpiti; each of these major segments figured prominently in the case, it being notable that the successor of Phatela's first house was Mpiti Sekake's most powerful supporter. These relationships are shown in figure 11. In the house of Phatela, Phalo is a major headman at Sekitsing ha Phalo, and Motloang at Sekitsing and Litsoeneng, both in the district of Mohale's Hoek and directly subject to the Principal Chief of Phamong. In the house of

Mpiti Mosothoane, Sejanamane is a headman at Malimong, and his senior brother Lisebo was his chief at Pheellong, where he was followed by his widow 'Mantsebo Seisa; Pheellong is in Qacha's Nek and is directly subject to the Principal Chief. In the house of Makoae, Kali (a main witness for Mitchell), though in the order of families from the sixth house of Sekake, described himself as Kali Makoae and conducted himself as a senior member of the Patlong chieftainship; he was acting chief after 'Mathabo's death, took a leading role in the meetings of the family, and was one of the four members of the Sekake-Makoae lineage to hold a major headmanship in Patlong (at Maboloka). The other major headmen in Patlong were (besides Mpiti himself at Thabana-Ts'ooana) Khanyetsi Malefane, headman of Thaba-Chitja, of Sekake's first house and son of Sehapa's younger brother in that house, and Makoko Sehapa, heir of Sehapa's second house, who was headman at Qhoalinyane and was succeeded by his son Mopeli Makoko.

The major decisions sketched in the preceding narrative were the work of the sons of Mosothoane, or such of them as were present. Questions of seniority arose but were not definitively resolved. Kali declared that he paid little attention to questions of seniority at the meetings. This remark, which he repeated and insisted on, is significant of the ambiguities that perplexed the decision-making body at the various stages of the dispute. These concern the two principles of seniority, the 'retrospective' and the 'circumspective', that were discussed at length in Chapter 2. In the present case, this takes the form of whether a relatively junior son of the house of Sekake is to be ranked above a senior son in the house of Phatela—whether, for example, Kali Makoae or Malefane Sekake is senior to Phalo Phatela. At a lower level of segmentation, a similar ambiguity surrounds the ranking of Orpen Maseru to Malefane or Khanyetsi, of Malefane to Makoko, and of Makoko to Sekake II. Phalo declares his seniority by reading his position as heir to the senior house in the major lineage next in order to Makoae; Kali however (who partly bases his claim on his years as well) has been promoted within the sons of Sekake, the senior segment of the whole Mosothoane lineage. Malefane, and his son Khanyetsi, come from the first house of Sekake Makoae, but Malefane was the junior son of that house; but precisely as junior son, he was full father's brother (*rangoane*) to Tautona, Sekake II and Makoko, and in that capacity a person of particular authority within the house of Sehapa after his elder brother's death. But Malefane's son is only a junior brother (patrilateral parallel cousin, to be exact) to Makoko, and the latter, as head of Sehapa's second house, played a leading role in the case, as indeed his son Mopeli did too.

As we have seen, Kali was reluctant to commit himself on general questions of seniority (his own position being rather difficult to account for in terms of any specific principle) and his reluctance was shared by other witnesses. There was a general tendency to stall or hedge when they were asked how many of the sons of Mosothoane were present on any one occasion, how many were considered to constitute a quorum, how the major segments aligned themselves in decision-making, and how relative seniority was defined. One way of arriving at a general estimate of the constitution of the 'family' starts from the assumption that when witnesses recite the names of persons who were present at a meeting or who took part in a decision, they will recall and name the most 'important' of the participants. Witnesses did, in fact, offer lists of names on many occasions (from three to about fifteen), and usually added some such phrase as 'and many others'. It is true that some of the witnesses were old and their memories might have been failing, but none the less there is sufficient consistency in the names recited to suggest that any erratic performances cancelled each other out and that the principal actors were recalled quite faithfully. It should also be remembered that some people who were major figures in earlier stages of the dispute were dead in 1952, so that their score in terms of mentions is low. In other cases, however, where a son or brother carried on in the place of an infirm or deceased man, the two voices speak as one. In addition to 'mentions' by witnesses, a score can be recorded for sons of Mosothoane who themselves appeared as witnesses in the case, and for those that the various Sotho courts singled out as being seniors. On this basis, some indicative assessment can be reached.

If the 'mentions' are summed (casual references and mere repetitions being excluded) they yield a total of 157 for the maximal lineage, the sons of Mosothoane. The detailed breakdown is as in table 1.

The sons of Sehapa thus account for about one quarter of the mentions, the sons of Sekake for about two-thirds, and those sons of Mosothoane who emerged from the two junior houses for about one quarter. It is clear, therefore, that the sons of Sekake constituted much the largest bloc, not only in terms of mentions, but also of the

TABLE I

A. Sons of Sehapa (four persons)			Total	Cumulative
1st house	Sekake II	6		
2nd house	Makoko 7⎫			
	Mopeli 15⎭	22		
	Shakhane	10	38	38
B. Sons of Sekake (ten persons)				
1st house	*Sons of Sehapa*	38		
	Malefane 5⎫			
	Khanyetsi 8⎭	13		
2nd house	Maseru 3⎫			
	Orpen 3⎭	6		
6th house	Kali 20⎫			
	Molaoli 8⎭	28		
9th house	Ntepe	8		
10th house	Matsepe	6		
?? house	Ralilochane	5		
	L. S. Makoae	1	67	105
C. Sons of Makoae (?) (four persons)				
1st house	*Sons of Sekake*	105		
?? house	Sekake Posholi	9		
	Phalo Posholi	1		
	Matsepe Posholi	1		
	Mosothoane			
	Posholi	1	12	117
D. Sons of Mosothoane (five persons)				
1st house	*Sons of Makoae*	117		
2nd house	Phalo Phatela	16		
	Mpiti Phatela	7		
	Motloang Phatela	10		
?? house	Mpoea Phatela	1		
3rd house	Sejanamane			
	Mphahama Mpiti	6	40	157

numbers of persons implicated (fourteen out of twenty-three). Phalo Phatela, however, the head of Mosothoane's second house, is a clear exception to this, as is Motloang Phatela from Phatela's second house. Moreover other sons of Mosothoane were not excluded: Sejanamane Mphahama Mpiti is mentioned a few times, and was a witness for the defendants, and other sons of Phatela are remembered and named by witnesses on both sides. One particular advantage that attached to the sons of Sekake was that they were so numerous. Sekake had eleven houses, only two of which failed to produce male issue. Moreover, they had the advantage, in many cases, of living either on the spot or in the general area of Patlong.

In the case before the Special Court, the two 'family' witnesses for the plaintiff were Mpiti himself and Phalo Phatela. The defendants called Mitchell, Kali, Molaoli (sixth house of Sekake, junior to Kali), Matsepe (tenth house of Sekake), Ntepe (ninth house of Sekake), Motloang Phatela (junior to Phalo), Sejanamane (a junior in the house of Mpiti Mosothoane) and Mopeli Makoko, from Sehapa's second house. Mpiti claimed, in general terms, that the defendants' witnesses were all 'juniors'. He chose to operate with a highly 'retrospective' frame of reference, since this alone would enable the support that he derived from Phalo to be reckoned as sufficiently senior, on its own, to avail against the seven family witnesses supporting his rival. But, from one point of view at least, Mpiti's whole case was retrospective, in that it depended on the view that on Tautona's death the line of succession should be located by going up to Sekake I, and then down again through Sekake II. Furthermore, Mpiti founded his case, for obvious reasons, upon an assertion of the strictness of the law governing chiefly succession, as against the characteristically 'circumspective' view that it is, up to a point, open to a chief to start the process of calculating seniority afresh. At the same time, he was ready, of course, to derive what support he could from the alternative argument that the defendants' backing came from junior lines, albeit within the senior segment of the maximal lineage.

The final aspect of the case to be considered concerns the relationship between the political and the lineage structure of Patlong ward. If the somewhat anomalous case of Kali at Maboloka is left aside, the political structure of the ward is reflected in the first four houses reading from left to right at the lowest level of figure 12, namely, Tautona/Mitchell, Sekake II/Mpiti, Makoko/Mopeli, and Malefane/Khanyetsi. The first and last of these are distributed, therefore, between the two sons of Sekake Makoae's first house, the first son naturally taking precedence over the second. The third represents the caretaking allotted to Sehapa's second house, and the second of them the ward allotted to Tautona's younger brother within the first house of Sehapa. Thereafter, the succession has followed from father to son and will, most probably, continue to do so. This means that junior sons will be edged out of the chiefly system, if minor caretakings cannot be found for them within the existing wards; but this latter provision is possible only within certain limits, since once a jurisdictional plenum has been reached, one of two results must follow: either the new chief acts as his predecessor did, and 'circumspectively' advances his own *immediate* agnates (in which case the former incumbents, from parallel but in lineage terms now junior lines, are extruded); or else the pattern of lineage seniority once set up is left intact, in which case the immediate agnates of any given chief, with the exception of his heir, relapse into commoner status. Mitchell's younger brothers in his own house, in fact, emerged as very obscure figures in the story of this dispute. It has taken Patlong some time to reach this position, and it may not quite have come to the end of the road even yet. This is due to the coincidence of two factors: the existence of a jurisdictional void in Qacha's Nek until its absorption into the general Koena system at the end of the last century, combined with the progressive settlement of the Orange River Valley, where Patlong lies. The significance of this is that it is not only, or even so much, land area that sets a limit on jurisdiction, but rather the numbers of potential subjects. While there is nothing to be gained in becoming chief of an uninhabited rock-face, on the other hand if settlement is dense as in relative terms it is in the Orange Valley, many jurisdictions can be supported. But once even this limit has been reached, a former chiefly family will be left with only one installed successor; the junior sons may act as counsellors or as village *liphala*,[9] but *their* junior sons will cease to be even that. Until recently, this process of progressive deterioration was accelerated by the placing system, which, as we have seen in Chapter 2, had the effect of depressing all subordinate levels whenever a senior chief was placed (see figure 5). But even now that disruptive placings have virtually ceased, there is little room left for the continued expansion of chieftainship, and it remains to be seen how Lesotho and its chiefs will cope with the resulting situation. It seems that chieftainship in Lesotho was in terms of its structural processes an intrinsically transitional institution, well adapted for purposes of expansion and the progressive settlement of unoccupied or conquered areas, but caught up in internal contradictions once such development had come to an end. The closure of the political frontiers in the last third of the nineteenth century walled up the only avenue of escape (Atmore 1969: 300f.), though it was only with the passing of several generations that pressures built up sufficiently to precipitate the attempts of the colonial government to control the situation in 1938.

Appendix 2 *The Laws of Lerotholi*

The following extracts have been taken from the 1959 edition of the *Laws of Lerotholi*, Part I. The English translation (as given in Duncan 1960) has been slightly modified.

Declaration of Basuto law and custom

Authority of the Paramount Chief

1. Under the authority which the Paramount Chief has according to Basuto law and custom, the Paramount Chief has full power and authority over every Mosotho resident in Lesotho.

Succession to chieftainship

2. The succession to chieftainship shall be by right of birth: that is the first born male child of the first wife married; if the first wife has no male issue then the first born male child of the next wife married in succession shall be the chief.

Provided that if a chief dies leaving no male issue the chieftainship shall devolve upon the male following according to the succession of houses.

Deceased chief leaving heir who is a minor

3. (1) If a chief dies leaving a minor son the senior widow or the younger brother of the deceased chief may act as chief during the minority of such son, and when that son ceases to be a minor the widow or the younger brother shall give place to him.

Allocation of land

7. (1) *Allocation of land generally*: Every chief and every headman . . . is responsible, within his area of jurisdiction, for the allocation of

land to his subjects. It shall be the duty of the chief and headman to see that land is allocated fairly and impartially.

(2) *Inspection of land allocated for the growing of crops*: Every chief and every headman . . . shall frequently inspect all lands . . . in his area . . . and is empowered to take away land from people who in his opinion have more lands than are necessary for their and their families' subsistence and grant such land . . . to his subjects who have no land or insufficient lands.

(3) *Deprivation of land not used or ill used*: It will be at the discretion of such chief or headman to take away a land or lands which he has allocated to any of his subjects who, through continued absence or insufficient reason, fails for two successive years properly to cultivate it or cause it to be cultivated.

(4) *Retention of lands by widows*: No widow shall be deprived of her land except under the provisions of paragraphs (2) and (3) above.

(5) *Provision of lands for minors and other sons on the death of their parents*:

(a) On the death of the father or mother, whoever dies last, all arable land allocated to them shall be regarded as land that has become vacant and shall revert to the chief or headman for re-allocation. However, should there be minor dependants left in such household, it shall be the duty of the guardian . . . to report their presence to the chief or headman, and it shall be the duty of the chief or headman to make provision for such minor dependants, during the period of their minority, from the land or lands of their deceased parents. If the minor dependants are sons, the chief or headman shall, on such sons attaining majority, confirm them on the land or lands.

(b) In the re-allocation of lands which have reverted to the chief or headman on the death of the previous occupier and after the needs of any minor dependants have been satisfied . . . the chief or headman shall give priority, in allocating any remaining lands, to the requirements of any adult son or sons of the deceased.

(c) Any person aggrieved by the action of the chief or headman . . . may complain to the Principal or Ward Chief . . . and if dissatisfied . . . he may appeal to the Paramount Chief. . . .

(7) *Land allocation for gardens and tree plantations, etc.*: On the death of a person who has been allocated the use of land for the growing of vegetables . . . or for the purpose of planting . . . or for

residential purposes, the heir, or in the absence of the heir, the dependants of such deceased person shall be entitled to the use of such land so long as he or they continue to dwell thereon.

(8) *Land required in the public interest*: Except in the public interest it shall not be lawful for any person to be deprived of his lands, gardens or tree plantations except in accordance with the provisions of this law. . . .

Heir

11. (1) The heir in Lesotho shall be the first male child of the first married wife, and if there is no male in the first house then the first born male child of the next wife married in succession shall be the heir.

(2) If there is no male issue in any house the senior widow shall be the heir, but according to the custom she is expected to consult the relatives of her deceased husband who are her proper advisers.

Minor heir

12. (1) When a man dies leaving a minor heir, the person appointed as guardian . . . shall keep a written record of the administration of the estate, and this record shall be open to inspection by the paternal uncles and other relatives of the heir permitted to do so under Basuto law.

(2) No property of the estate shall be sold or otherwise disposed of by the guardian . . . or widow without the prior consent of the paternal uncles and other relatives of the heir.

(3) If the heir in any house is a minor, the principal heir [sc., the heir of the senior house], if he is of age, is regarded as his guardian.

(4) Where property has been allocated to any particular house and the wife in that house predeceases her husband, the property allocated shall remain with that house to be inherited on the death of the father by the eldest son of that house and to be shared by him with his junior brothers in his own house according to Basuto law and custom.

Inheritance

13. (1) Subject to the provisions of paragraph 14 the heir in Lesotho shall inherit all the unallocated property of the estate and he

CL—K*

is obliged by custom to use the estate with his father's widow or
widows and to share with his junior brothers according to their rank,
which shall be according to the order in which their mothers were
married.

(2) The question of what portion of the unallocated estate shall be
set aside for the support of the deceased's widow or widows ... shall
be decided by the paternal uncles of the principal heir and other
persons whose right it is.

Allocation of property during lifetime

14.   (1) If a man during his lifetime allots his property amongst his
various houses but does not distribute such property ... his wishes
must be carried out, provided the heir ... has not been deprived of
the greater part of his father's estate.

(2) A widow who has no male issue in her house shall have the use
of all the property allocated to her house. On her death the principal
heir shall inherit the remaining property but he must use it for the
maintenance of any dependants in that house; provided that no
widow may dispose of any of the property without the prior consent
of her guardian.

(3) If there is male issue in any house ... the widow shall have the
use of all the property allocated to her house and at her death any
property remaining shall devolve upon the eldest son of her house
who must share such property with his junior brothers in his house;
provided that no widow may dispose of any property without consultation with the guardian while that son is a minor, and provided
further that on reaching his majority the eldest son will assume control of the property in his house.

(4) Any dispute among the deceased's family over property or
property rights shall be referred for arbitration to the brothers of
the deceased and to the other persons entitled to be consulted.

List of cases cited

Bk   *Masopha* v. *Mabu*   JC 261/48
Bl   *Masopha* v. *Rapopo*   JC 22/64
Bm   *Mathealira* v. *Tumo*   JC 135/51
Bn   *Matjatumile* v. *Khale*   JC 237/54
Bo   *Matjeketjela* v. *Theko*   JC 19/47
Bp   *'Matli* v. *Letsie*   JC 4/49
Bq   *Matsela* v. *Matete*   JC 243/60
Br   *'Matsoana* v. *'Matsoana*   JC 85/45
Bs   *Matsosa* v. *Matsosa*   JC 151/55; AC I Matsieng CC 190/55
Bt   *Motsoso* v. *Motsoso*   JC 247/63
Bu   *Mojake* v. *Litjamela*   JC 4/63
Bv   *Mokola* v. *Klaas*   JC 243/64
Bw   *Mokonyana* v. *Motumi*   JC 102/61
Bx   *Moleko* v. *Motsumi*   JC 3/58
By   *Monne* v. *Ralienyane*   JC 570/52
Bz   *Monyana* v. *Ralilochane*   JC 128/61
Ca   *Moqa* v. *Moqa*   JC 206/49
Cb   *Morie* v. *Mokhesi*   JC 211/64
Cc   *Mosoeunyane* v. *Khomoeamollo*   JC 27/61
Cd   *Mosothoane* v. *Malefane*   JC 17/59
Ce   *Mothibeli* v. *Lesaoana*   JC 52/50
Cf   *Motjoli* v. *Rametse*   JC 106/58
Cg   *Motlamelle* v. *Lerata*   JC 172/57
Ch   *Mphuthing* v. *Kubutona*   JC 23/66
Ci   *Mthembu* v. *Monare*   JC 272/63
Cj   *Ndlaba* v. *Qhobela*   JC 111/65
Ck   *Njeke* v. *Tanthiba*   JC 61/59
Cl   *Nkhasi* v. *Mansel*   JC 241/53
Cm   *Nthathakane* v. *Nthathakane*   JC 78/44
Cn   *Ntholi* v. *Selebalo*   JC 75/56
Co   *Ntoala* v. *Morake*   JC 227/60
Cp   *Phakisi* v. *Borena*   JC 69/54
Cq   *Phatela* v. *Mapote*   JC 163/49
Cr   *Qatha* v. *Nte*   JC 55/64; Likoeneng Central CC 49/63
Cs   *Rakhoboso* v. *Nkaka*   JC 49/51
Ct   *Ralienyane* v. *Lekaota*   JC 11/62
Cu   *Ramabanda* v. *Nkopane*   JC 134/45
Cv   *Rankali* v. *Thelelisane*   JC 162/60
Cw   *Rannana* v. *Sehloho*   JC 194/55
Cx   *Seeisa* v. *Ntsoereng*   JC 31/45
Cy   *Seisa* v. *Seisa*   JC 80/62
Cz   *Sekake* v. *Tautona*   JC 15/59
Da   *Setsapa* v. *Lethuoa*   JC 125/64
Db   *Thipane* v. *Thipane*   JC 183/60
Dc   *Tlapi* v. *Mosoabi*   JC 217/53
Dd   *Tsikoane* v. *Thella*   JC 92/52

Notes

Introduction: Aims and methods

1 The best general accounts are Ashton 1967, Hailey 1953, Halpern 1965, Spence 1968; see also Stevens 1967. Reservations about Ashton and Stevens are expressed in Hamnett 1967a. The leading studies by social anthropologists are Ashton 1938, 1946 and 1967, Jones 1951 and 1966, Sheddick 1953 and 1954, Wallman 1969. The only general work expressly on Sotho customary law is Duncan 1960; this is a serviceable handbook for lawyers by a former Judicial Commissioner with a fluent knowledge of Sesotho and an intimate knowledge of Lesotho, but it displays too great a deference to the views of European judges to be entirely acceptable from a social anthropological point of view. Other legal studies are Palmer 1970, Palmer and Poulter 1972, Ramolefe n.d., 1969 and 1970.

2. The Basutoland National Party (BNP), though not of recent origin, only rose to prominence in the year or so preceding the General Election of 1965. It was alleged to have received financial and other help from South Africa. The Congress (BCP) was said to have been financed from Peking and the royalist MFP from Moscow. Very shortly after the election, Congress and the MFP entered into a close alliance against the Government, and at the same time an open quarrel developed between the King and the Prime Minister which persisted into independence and beyond. The best accounts of recent political events are Halpern, 1965, Spence 1968 and Weisfelder 1969, 1972a, 1972b. A strongly pro-Government view is in Proctor 1969.

3 I am very grateful to Professor P. H. Gulliver for pointing out the contentious nature of the aspects of method discussed in this section and suggesting that they should be explicitly justified.

4 The standard Southern Sotho-English dictionary is by Paroz 1961; grammars are Doke and Mofokeng 1957 and Paroz 1957. The classic general account of Southern Bantu languages is Doke 1954.

The stem *-sotho* is pronounced somewhat as English 'soo-too'.

1 Customary law

1 See also Mair 1962: 19, and some pertinent remarks in Gulliver 1969a: 12–13.

2 See Gluckman 1955: 239–40.

3 Gluckman's conceptualisation of legal rules as hierarchically ordered and thus not all of equivalent value is relevant here (1955: 295).

4 Thus, Fallers aptly remarks that 'saying that custom is a *source* of law is not the same as saying that custom *is* law' (1969: 66, original italics). See also p. 107 below.

5 Cf. Gluckman 1955: 231ff., 253–4.

6 Gluckman in several places stresses how, in his view, one of the main goals of the Lozi courts is to reconcile rather than simply to adjudicate. 'Reconciliation of the parties becomes one of the main aims of the judges when the parties are in a relationship which it is valuable to preserve; and to achieve this aim requires a broadening of enquiry and hence of the concept of "relevant evidence". But this aim does not lead' (he is careful to note) 'to a sacrifice of legal and moral rules' (1955: 78). Adam Kuper, in his study of the Kgalagari, has suggested that conciliation is precisely the function of relatively high-level courts, such as those which Gluckman principally studied. Face-to-face tribunals (like the Kgalagari *lekgota*) must, he says, rely on 'objectivity and strict legalism' (1970: 164). In a subsequent paper (Kuper 1971) he has elaborated and generalised this argument, and given some consideration to Faller's discussion of 'legalism'. The issue, however, is far from settled and calls for much fuller debate. The present study makes no direct contribution to this most interesting problem.

7 Fallers in fact qualifies this description by describing Soga tribunals as 'in some degree' true courts of law, but these words seem unnecessary, and indeed inconsistent with the general line of argument, and for that reason they have been omitted.

8 Gulliver has subsequently published rather different formulations (1969a), but the original discussion still stands as an analytical starting-point of great utility. See also Moore 1970.

9 See similar comments in Moore 1970: 324.

10 See Moore 1970: 323. However, she stresses the 'discretionary' element in the (inevitable) departure of judges from the mechanical application of rules. I prefer to stress the *legitimacy* of alternative outcomes.

11 Cf. Gluckman 1955: 27, 51, 69, 70.

2 The public law of chieftainship succession

1 Much of the material in this chapter has been published in Hamnett 1965. I am much indebted to Mr Makhaola Lerotholi's criticism of that article; however, I maintain my general argument, and for this Mr Lerotholi, as a convinced 'retrospectivist', would be the first to disclaim responsibility. See also note 10 below.

2 The best general historical account is Ellenberger and MacGregor 1912, but see also Lagden 1909 and Wilson and Thompson 1969. Tylden 1950 may also be consulted. Other studies of particular aspects of Sotho history are by Atmore, Legassick and Lye (all in Thompson 1969) and Jones 1966. Brief historical sketches are in Ashton 1967, Hailey 1953 and Jones 1951. A popular but acceptable life of

Moshoeshoe I is Becker 1969. Historical materials are in *Basutoland Notes and Records* (*passim*) and Germond 1967.

3 Professor Edward Batson, Director of the 1956 Social Survey of Basutoland, has in a private communication informed me that the proportion of male heads of households described as 'Kwena' in the 1956 Social Survey was thirty per cent.

4 See below, note 8.

5 The circumstances are narrated later in this chapter, pp. 39–40.

6 The two Principal Chiefdoms are those associated with the Khoakhoa and the Taung peoples. The Tlokoa (in recognition of their loyalty to the Koena during the Gun war of 1880–81) enjoyed a similar autonomy until 1925, when Paramount Chief Griffith placed his son Seeiso over the Tlokoa chief, Lelingoana. This appointment led to a long dispute, which was only resolved in 1948, when Lelingoana's son Mosuoe was recognised as 'chief of the Tlokoa' with the special status of Ward Chief. The Tlokoa ward was still subject to the Principal Chief of Mokhotlong, but since the latter was in fact the Paramount Chief himself, the settlement was a fair compromise. See *Lelingoana v. P.C.* JC 31/46.

7 Jurisdiction is not, in fact, quite as rigorous territorially as this suggests. A major source of jurisdictional anomalies lies in the institution of *paballo* (now officially eliminated) whereby one chief could borrow administrative rights in a neighbouring ward. This topic is of great technical complexity and cannot be considered in the present work. 'Inter-ploughing' is another complicating factor that must be omitted here. See Sheddick 1954: 139ff., and Hamnett 1970: Chapter 4. In the present context, these irregularities of jurisdiction can be safely ignored.

8 One instance among many: early in this century, a son of Moshoeshoe's brother Makhabane came south from Mapoteng to Matelile and was placed as Koena Chief over the existing Taung chief, Raborabane; the Raborabane lineage is now represented only by an un-gazetted headman — virtually a mere herald (*phala*) — in the village of Thabaneng.

9 This point is stressed by Atmore (1969: 300f.).

10 In my earlier article (Hamnett 1965: 245) I suggested that Leshoboro's act in pouring soil on to Mojela's grave was evidence of his national seniority. In fact, this pouring of the soil referred to internal relationships within the deceased's lineage; Leshoboro poured soil in his capacity as senior father's sister's son. The Paramount Chief poured first, then Leshoboro, and nobody else poured at all. This avoided any unpleasantness when it came to ranking the other members of the Letsie lineage in relation to other cardinal lines. (Sometimes a relatively unimportant person with no plausible claim to a senior position in the lineage will be invited to pour, to avoid quarrels over a grave.) I am indebted to Mr Makhaola Lerotholi for correcting my mistake on this point, and also for pointing out the misleading implication in my reference (1965: 246) to the Chief of Boleka. The case of this

'junior royal' shows that even on the most 'circumspective' principle, a very junior scion of the senior segment could not be promoted over another cardinal line; the demographic and economic factors referred to at the foot of p. 245 have no direct relevance.

11 Cf. 'A résumé of the causes which have led to the present condition of affairs in the Leribe district', anonymous MS., Lesotho Archives, Maseru. Dr A. Atmore in a private communication has suggested that the author is probably the historian and folklorist, Azariele Sekese.

12 The Paramount Chief enjoyed an appellate jurisdiction over the whole country, especially in disputes between Principal Chiefs, or between a Principal Chief and a subordinate. He also possessed general authority over boundary disputes, and there are many examples of his intervention outside the Letsie provinces, including in the Molapo ward, e.g., *Tsikoane* v. *Thella* JC 92/52, *Ketisi* v. *Neisi* JC 215/54. A further instance concerns the ward of Koeneng and Mapoteng; this was originally a loan (*paballo*) made by the Molapo chiefs to Lesaoana, the son of Moshoeshoe's brother Makhabane, but it was converted into a ward in its own right by the Paramount Chief; this was something quite close to an invasion of Molapo rights.

It is also the case that in terms both of population and of geographical area, Letsie's house commands the greater part of Lesotho. This reflects the fact that the original wards of the sons of Moshoeshoe did not extend to cover the whole territory now comprised by Lesotho; when other areas were brought within the nation (Mokhotlong, Qacha's Nek, Quthing and Mohale's Hoek) they were annexed to the Paramountcy and later distributed among the sons of Letsie. Had the expansion taken place in the north, in Molapo country, the subsequent history of Lesotho might have been very different.

13 Nehemiah was the sixth of all the sons of Moshoeshoe, a child of the third house. In his second house, Moshoeshoe had one son. Nehemiah claimed that the third house—that of the 'wife of the breast'—took precedence not only over the second, but also over all but the eldest son of the first house (Moshesh 1880). There seems little to support this view.

14 See Jones 1966.

15 The 'family council' is discussed in greater detail in Chapter 3, pp. 49–50.

16 It is widely believed that Chief Goliath Moshoeshoe, a son of Moshoeshoe through the female line, entered into a leviratic union with a widow of Letsie II, and that Makhaola Letsie (born 1918) is the fruit of this union.

17 These issues were fully canvassed in *Sekake* v. *Tautona* JC 15/59, of which a full account is given in Appendix 1.

18 Thus the author of the narrative referred to in note 10 above. Some opponents of the present King have argued that he should not have succeeded since his mother is of Tlokoa origin (see note 6 above).

The ranking applies especially to the first three houses; subsequent wives are separated by a wider gulf.

19 It could be maintained that a chieftainship system such as that of

Lesotho is an essentially transitional institution, well adapted for the purposes of 'predatory expansion' (cf. Sahlins 1961) but bound to founder on internal contradictions once development and settlement have come to an end. This argument is elaborated in Appendix 1.

20 It will, however, be argued subsequently that this polarity is not exhaustive of the categories in which Sotho law can best be analysed.

21 One notable case not explicitly cited in this chapter but generally relevant to much of it is the co-called Regency Case, *Bereng* v. *'Mantsebo* 1926–53 HCTLR 50.

3 The law of private succession and inheritance

1 The phrase literally means 'lands of the enemy'. These are annexed to the chieftainship as such and their identity remains constant. Strictly speaking, only Principal Chiefs have chieftainship fields. They were traditionally worked by tribute labour and still often are; in theory, they provide the wherewithal for the discharge of chiefly obligations to widows, orphans, strangers, and so on, and as a reserve resource for the people of the ward.

2 'The links of a family are unbreakable from generation to generation', as Ezekias argued in a case against his nephew's widow: *Labone* v. *Lichaba* JC 334/49. The Paramount Chief's Court reminded Makhaola, the leviratic issue of Goliath mentioned in Chapter 2, note 16, that 'your father is still alive, in the person of Paramount Chieftainess 'Mantsebo' (*Makhaola* v. *Bolae* JC 182/64). The Paramount Chief's Court again described one young man as the father of his paternal grandmother, his father and his father's father both being dead (*Lichaba* v. *Lekata* JC 7/44).

3 I am thinking largely of the bewilderment of the European Courts and their clumsiness (albeit well-intentioned) in this area; but the puzzlement is also apparent in the treatment this tract of law has received outside the courts and away from the bench (e.g., Duncan 1960, Ramolefe 1969).

4 Continental jurists, with their experience of codes and their different approach to *la jurisprudence*, are better equipped, paradoxically enough, for the understanding of customary law than are English and South African lawyers, with their case-law orientation. Customary law is not nearly so close to case-law as it is to a system possessing what could be called an 'implicit code'.

5 Cf. the cognate Lozi *bung'a* discussed in Gluckman 1955: 191, 200. It might be as well to recall here the point, familiar to students of jurisprudence, that 'ownership' is in any case little more than a shorthand term to describe a 'bundle of rights', whose exact composition varies from society to society. 'Ownership' is not a concept capable of universal definition.

6 I cannot recall any Mosotho of whom I could say that he had never been involved in a 'case' (*nyeoe*). A very large number had either past or present experience of some kind of litigation or dispute. The word

nyeoe is used to describe any kind of claim or plea, whether administrative or judicial in current definition; but this only goes to show the wide range of matters that Basotho assimilate to litigable disputes.

7 One objection to the concept of usufruct is that it implies a unique (natural or legal) person as owner; such a person could only be the agnatic corporation, so that the term is misused if it is employed to define an individual owner within the lineage. Another objection is that it implies a disjunction between a capital resource and its fruits; this is misleading inasmuch as a 'usufructuary' may be entitled to use and even dispose of (e.g.) a herd, or of parts of it other than its 'fructus'.

8 Ultimately no doubt a metalanguage of comparative jurisprudence is the only answer (cf. Vanderlinden 1966 and 1969).

9 Cf. Gluckman's remarks on the different weighting given to legal rules that may not be fully consistent with each other (1955: 202, 283, 298, 305).

10 The word *lekhotla*, besides meaning 'court' in the judicial and administrative senses, is also used of any deliberative assembly (e.g., the National Council) and in addition can be applied to a band or regiment of warriors, or to a political party.

11 As we shall see, the task of judicial courts is (officially) to *ascertain* rights, not to create them.

12 *Manyebutse* v. *Manyebutse* (Bi), judgment of Paramount Chief's Court (note the Salomonic touch).

13 A distinction exists in modern Sesotho usage between a (judicial) judgment (*kahlolo*) and an administrative decision (*khaolo*). Sometimes the difference is emphasised; the Paramount Chief's administrative court defended itself against judicial appeal by insisting that 'this is not a judgment, it is a decision' (Cq). But in *'Matsoana* (Br) the court's opinion was headed 'Judgment' (*Kahlolo*) but ended with the words 'this is the decision' (*khaolo*). Such inconsistency is a feature of the transition through which the courts are passing.

14 It is true that George distinguishes between the case where a widow has a son and the case where she does not, and this might seem to give special meaning to his statement that in the absence of male issue the widow 'inherits' the cattle, especially as he qualifies the son's 'inheriting' (where there is male issue) by saying that he is only 'acting for his mother, who has charge . . . during her lifetime . . . but at her death, then it devolves upon' the heir of the house. Since the widow inherits in a qualified sense where there is a son, then where there is no son, her inheritance must (apparently) be unqualified, giving her the right of disposal. But this argument, though plausible, is unsound. Where there is a son, George first states that he 'inherits' and then proceeds to qualify the rights which this confers to a point which seems to restore effective control to the widow. Where there is no son, the matter cannot be expressed in quite this way, and the widow is therefore said to 'inherit'. But it is quite certain that in George's time widows (in common with women in general) were obliged to act always and only 'with' the male agnates of the deceased, and the core of the doctrine remains: the agnatic family cannot be deprived of its wealth by the unilateral

act of a widow, who (after all) remains married to her deceased husband's family even after his death.

The relevant passage comes from the *Report and Evidence of the Commission on Native Laws and Customs of the Basuto*, Cape Town, 1873, 3 December 1872, paragraph 21. The quotation as printed in Duncan 1960: 11 contains a misprint. As the Judicial Commissioner observed in *Khatala* v. *Khatala* JC 70/61, the word 'and' in the last sentence should read 'who'; the error entirely reverses the sense.

15 A widow is entitled to the same standard of living as she enjoyed in her husband's lifetime: Thabana-Morena Court in *Leluma* v. *Mojela* JC 184/64.

16 There is really a kind of guardianship within guardianship that so to speak reverses back on itself. The widow, as we have seen, holds the estate that she can use only 'for' the house; yet the son is (if married, at least) his mother's guardian too. He looks after the cattle 'for' his mother, who in turn looks after them 'for' him.

17 Polygamy (*sethepu*) is comparatively uncommon today. Using data from the 1956 Census, it can be calculated that only about 4 per cent of males and 7 per cent of females were partners in polygamous marriages, and in most cases there were only two wives. These figures should almost certainly be reduced today. Nevertheless, the law concerning 'houses' remains of great importance for a number of reasons. (1) Many contemporary disputes about inheritance and succession depend upon issues of fact relating to a period when polygamy was common. (2) Chiefs have traditionally been polygamous and it is above all in the chieftainship that many crucial issues of seniority arise with consequences reaching out beyond the direct successors and affecting the junior sons of junior sons. (3) Customary law marriages are still, it can be argued, polygamous, though it may be a case of 'polygamy with one wife'. The law that applies to succession, inheritance and filiation reflects a polygamous society. (4) Basotho often apply categories derived from polygamy to situations which might not be so regarded in modern courts. For instance, when a man remarries after divorce, or after the death of his wife, the rules applying to 'houses' are often invoked (*Lephole* v. *Lephole* JC 15/58, *Ntoula* v. *Morake* JC 227/60, *Mojake* v. *Litjamela* JC 4/63). (5) The rules about 'houses' are not seldom applied between full brothers as well as between half-brothers, and especially to the children of full brothers (*Mojake* v. *Litjamela*, above).

In these senses, polygamy and the rules of polygamy are still very relevant factors in current disputes.

18 The main line of cases is *Makupu* v. *Makupu* JC 89/55, *Ralienyane* v. *Lekaota* JC 11/62, *Seisa* v. *Seisa* JC 80/62 and *Khatala* v. *Khatala* JC 70/61. (The Appeal Court judgment in *Khatala* is reported in *Journal of African Law*, 10, 3, Autumn 1966: 173–7.) I do not find Ramolefe's discussion of the issue (1969) either helpful or accurate.

19 The view of reasoned decision adopted here follows the thesis in Louch 1966.

20 Cf. Sawer 1965: 105, and the discussion of 'declaratory law' on pages 102 ff.
21 Cf. Gluckman 1955: 310, 'the certainty of the law . . . is maintained through what is clearly chanciness in litigation'.

4 Land tenure

1 This simple statement leaves aside the question of *paballo* (the loan of administrative titles) referred to in Chapter 2, note 7 above.
2 As we shall see, the chief or headman in his turn should allocate land through the agency of his appointed land-issuers (*baabi*).
3 Sheddick excludes any Roman-Dutch connotations in using this term.
4 The matter of chieftainship fields is left out of account in this context; see Chapter 3, note 1 and text, p. 45.
5 Thus, a man cannot owe allegiance to two chiefs at once (sc., of equivalent jurisdictional level). The question of *paballo* (see note 1 above) is once again left aside.
6 Against Sheddick (1954: 183–92) I maintain the view that there is a serious land shortage in Lesotho. See Hamnett 1973a.
7 Subjects participate in these disputes, however, since their usufructuary titles depend on the chief's right to allocate.
8 Basotho do not, as a rule, attach much importance to particular parcels of arable land. Their attitude to such land is basically instrumental, and a man who could exchange a poor land for a good one would be unlikely to refuse out of any attachment to 'his father's' lands. The stress on the family lands is a practical one. The identity of a given land also has evidential importance, however, since it is usually easier to support a claim to be the entitled occupier if it can be shown that a land has been 'in the family' for some years and ploughed by a particular person. Consequently, considerable importance is attached to particular land-parcels, but the reason for this should not be misunderstood. It is otherwise with residential sites, to which there is considerable attachment. When a site changes hands, usually after a death, the new owner fears magical attack at the hands of the dead man's lineage. The former owner will have (or will be thought to have) hidden medicines under the hut which will be dangerous to any stranger. The new owner will often destroy the hut and build a new one in a different place. Similarly, when a man alienates a site, he opens himself to reprisals from his own ancestors; and if on marriage he moves to his wife's place, he will be nervous about supernatural dangers unless some months pass without any untoward accidents. (It is true that medicines are also used on lands, but this is to protect the fertility of the soil against possible magic or witchcraft from a neighbour.)
9 For all quantified estimates of land use, etc., see Morojele 1962.
10 When a right is subject to a resolutive condition, it is effective unless and until the condition is fulfilled. Under a suspensive condition, the right vests only when the condition is fulfilled.
11 *Morie* v. *Mokhesi* JC 211/64. The Central Court at Matsieng stated

that 'loan of land does not exist in our law. . . . It is not true that a person can be allocated a land temporarily.' This is probably to overstate the matter, but in *Morie*, the loan was alleged to be of twenty-three years' duration.

12 One informant told me that on his father's death, 'I took one of my father's lands and made my lands up to three. I gave two lands to my brother, and he got a third from the chief'; but further discussion made it quite clear that the words 'I took', 'I gave', were elliptical, and that the chief's active consent and collaboration were involved throughout.

13 Two women will enter a trading store, the one to sell corn and the other to buy it; the trader takes a profit of up to 20 per cent. Two women in the same household are less likely to have to resort to this kind of transaction.

14 W. A. Ramsden's judgments as Judicial Commissioner in *Ntholi* v. *Selebalo* JC 75/56 and *Khalime* v. *Lesaoana* JC 82/56 are distortions of Sotho law in this whole field. Cf. also his mis-reading of both Sotho and Roman law in *Lekulana* v. *P.C.* JC 108/56. See Hamnett 1971: 267–8.

15 'I find that these are lands of removers, your father and mother being dead', Paramount Chief's Court in *Manyeli* v. *Brand* JC 168/45.

16 Several proverbs describe a man who runs after two chiefs—'a needle with two points', 'a wagtail with a piebald tail', 'he eats with both jaws'.

17 Estimated at 0·4 per cent of all holdings (Morojele 1962).

18 An informant told me that his Principal Chief refused him permission to build a house on an arable field, saying that 'Lesotho must not be turned into a country of farms.'

19 Though I took no systematic count, I would estimate that about one-half of all cases appealed to the Judicial Commissioner involved disputes over lands.

20 The phrase is ubiquitous in Sotho judgments. The earliest explicit reference I came across was in a judgment of the Paramount Chief's Court in 1934 (see *Kekane* v. *Makhorole* JC 11/60).

5 Chiefs and the courts

1 I have considered a 'major' chief to be one who *either* (a) is directly subject to his Principal Chief, and has two or more gazetted chiefs or headmen subordinate to him *or* (b) if directly subject to a chief other than a Principal Chief, has three or more chiefs or headmen subordinate to him.

2 Casalis's comment (1930: 268–9) is perhaps unduly swayed by sentiment: 'Ce mot a une très belle origine. Il est formé du verbe *rêna*: être tranquille. *Morêna* signifie donc: celui qui veille à la sureté et au bien public'.

The word *mofumahali* (chieftainess) is formed from the stem -*fuma*, also meaning 'wealth'.

3 It is notable how easily the radical Congress Party were able to reverse

C L—L

their previously hostile stance to the Paramount Chief after the National Party's victory in the General Election of 1965. Whatever the real feelings of the intelligentsia, the rank and file were relieved to find that their support of Congress was no longer in conflict with their allegiance to the King.

4 This kind of loan is known as *mafisa*; for discussion see Ashton 1967: 181, Sheddick 1954: 109f., Duncan 1960: 81f., Morojele 1962: Parts 2 and 7, and Wallman 1969; 67. (Sandra Wallman seems to be mistaken in stating it as a general rule that the borrower becomes owner of the progeny.)

5 See Chapter 4, note 6 above.

6 For a list of Sotho proverbs and theoretical comment, see Hamnett 1967b.

7 Compare Gluckman 1955: 51, 69 70. The Basotho Courts, however, seem to have been less aware of the differentiation of function involved than were those of the Barotse (1955: 27).

8 For a systematic account of the court structure, see Palmer and Poulter 1972 and Ramolefe 1970. The general law of Lesotho is Roman-Dutch. For the reception of the law in force in Cape Colony on 2 February 1884, see also Poulter 1969 and Beardsley 1970.

9 The first distinction between 'judicial' and 'administrative' matters in the traditional sector seems to date from the early 1930s, having of course been imported from the colonial government.

10 In *Macolela* v. *Ntereke* JC 109/58 the Court diverted the onus from the claimant to the possessor of a disputed article. In *Mosothoane* v. *Malefane* JC 17/59 a violently evicted land-holder was required to sue his evictor. Cf. also *Matjatumile* v. *Khale* JC 237/54, where the plaintiff had a disputed beast in his possession and went to court to have his right affirmed.

11 'Large parts of the judgments read like sermons' (Gluckman 1955: 49).

12 The relationship between the judicial and administrative spheres creates profound intellectual as well as practical problems in modern jurisdictions. An outstanding discussion of the concept of 'justiciability' is in Marshall 1961. That the dilemma confronting administrative tribunals is an omnipresent one and not simply the result of Sotho inexperience may be seen from Shapiro 1965; arbitrary action may be struck down by the courts on the grounds that it is contrary to natural justice, but the establishment of rules and the following of previous decisions carry the risk that the court will quash the tribunal's findings on the ground that it has attempted to act 'judicially'. The difficulties seem more acute in the Anglo-American common-law jurisdictions than in the civilian and code-based continental systems, where the *droit administratif* and its analogues (so profoundly misunderstood by Dicey) have made possible an alternative approach (Dicey 1948: lxxi–xcv, 183–283; Wade 1961: 7f.). The common-law tradition has been to seek ever more delicate points of articulation between 'law' and 'discretion', providing different institutional structures for each and

linking them only at the level, and within the constraints, of review procedure.

Conclusion: Politics, administration and executive law

1 It is a distracting circumstance that the term 'administrative', when applied to a court in opposition to the term 'judicial', should fall into Smith's 'political' category, while the 'judicial' courts are 'administrative' in Smith's terms. However, the context should indicate the sense that the word 'administrative' is intended to bear when it occurs.

2 The discussion in Smith 1965 starts from different theoretical perspectives and has little bearing on the present argument.

3. Chapter 15.

4 For instance, Pound 1923, Stone 1964 and 1966: 50–85, Friedmann 1967: 436–514.

5 Yet some of the implications of the 'pure theory of law' come near it— Kelsen 1934.

   In the practice of the courts, some familiar pieces of jargon are highly redolent of a 'declaratory' view: 'If your Lordship so finds the law', 'the words that have fallen from your Lordship's mouth'.

6 Gluckman notes it for the Barotse (1955: 254).

7 Sir Henry Maine stressed the importance of the stage in legal and social development at which codification takes place. In Rome, it occurred at so early a point (the Twelve Tables are conventionally dated 451–450 BC) that change and growth overran the code, leaving it with only a formal dignity but without practical consequences. Maine suggests that it was because Hindu law was, if not codified, at least committed to writing, after it had developed certain 'cruel absurdities' that it acted as a powerfully conservative force (Maine 1950: 15–17).

8 Until the 1940s, District Commissioners enjoyed and not seldom exercised the powers of magistrates. This meant that they were in a position to issue orders in one capacity and punish those who disobeyed them in another. In a formal sense, they were like chiefs in this respect, but their actions carried little inherent legitimacy and they were regarded as part of the colonial 'government' in whichever capacity they acted.

9 The late Dr Nan Wilson is, so far as I know, the only social anthropologist to have conducted a full analytical study of a modern court and bar (Wilson 1965). Her thesis gives an excellent insight into the structure of professional roles in the day-to-day work of the Court of Session in Edinburgh and of the functional mechanisms that both segregate and interrelate them.

10 Cf. Gluckman 1955: 51, 230, 254.

11 For the rule against set-off, see e.g. *Rankali* v. *Thelelisane* JC 162/60, *Mosoeunyane* v. *Khomoeamollo* JC 27/61, *Mokonyana* v. *Motumi* JC 102/61, *Monyana* v. *Ralilochane* JC 128/61. The Judicial Commissioners normally upheld this rule, whose 'legalism' makes it congenial to the judicial courts, whereas they have been much more reluctant to enforce the rule against time-bar: *Mafisa* v. *Mots'oene* JC 305/49. In

Dimema v. *Velaphe* JC 5/45 the Judicial Commissioner even held that the creditor must prosecute his claim during his lifetime. In *Makibi* v. *Khoai* JC 83/57, he refused to consider a twenty-nine-year-old claim and adopted the doctrine that although the debt might not cease to be due, it could not be sued for after a certain time. (This is not so vacuous as it may sound, since if the creditor can at any time lawfully gain possession of what is owed, he can resist the debtor's claim for its restitution—i.e., the *naturalis obligatio* remains.) In *Njeke* v. *Ranthiba* JC 61/59 the Appeal Court at Matsieng refused to entertain a claim going back sixty years. Of course, in such cases the extreme difficulty of proof provides an obstacle to the claimant, and Basotho Courts might on occasion confuse the defeat of a claim on these grounds with its exclusion as a matter of *law*.

12 Customary law can perhaps be regarded as that sub-class of 'executive law' that prevails in the absence of writing and of a specialised judiciary. Ethnographically, it corresponds to the anthropological cluster designated as 'traditional monarchies' and is found in conjunction with an economy and a system of internal stratification marked by a limited degree of functional differentiation. Analytically, however, there is no reason to limit the general category of 'executive law' to this particular empirical case.

13 Review procedure usually concerns itself with whether a decision was made in good faith, and whether the criteria of *audiatur et altera pars* and *nemo sit iudex in causa sua* were adhered to. The remedy is normally to remit the matter for reconsideration by the competent authority rather than to substitute an alternative decision.

Appendix 1   Case study: the chieftainship dispute at Patlong

1 Some of the wider background to the case can be found in Jones 1966: 64ff., 74ff.

2 *Sekake* v. *Tautona* JC 15/59. The appellant was Mpiti Sekake, and the respondents Mitchell Tautona and his mother 'Mantoetse (see figure 13).

3 See p. 128 below. The succession returns to the agnatic line after the chieftainess's death.

4 Sc., posthumously *conceived* children, born to a leviratic union.

5 See Chapter 2 note 16.

6 See Chapter 4 note 10.

7 See Chapter 2 pp. 39–40.

8 Leenhardt (1939) states circumstantially and at length that the identity of individual cattle is actually constitutive of affinal relationships; however, I found no evidence that this was so and much that suggests the opposite. I am confirmed in my scepticism by the opinion privately expressed to me by the Sotho scholar, Rev. G. M. Setiloane. Leenhardt may have been generalising from a very local practice, or (more probably) misled by the *evidential* importance of recognising particular beasts into thinking that their identity actually constituted

relationships. If ego's wife's brother pays bridewealth cattle to marry his younger brother to a woman from a third family, ego's relationship to that third family (*viz.*, to his wBwF) does not depend on whether or not the cattle paid over to it by his wife's brother came from ego's kraal.

9 'Bugles', i.e., the delegates or appointed spokesmen of a chief or headman. These are not hereditary offices but depend on the chief's patronage. A chief may have a *phala* in an outlying hamlet within his ward, but he often appoints one in his own village to call meetings and make announcements, or perhaps to speak on the chief's behalf even when the chief is there himself.

References

ALLOTT, A. N. (1960) *Essays in African Law* (first edition). London: Butterworths.

ALLOTT, A. N. (ed.) (1970) *Judicial and Legal Systems in Africa* (second edition). London: Butterworths.

ASHTON, E. H. (1938) 'Political organisation of the Southern Sotho', *Bantu Studies* 12, 4: 287–320.

ASHTON, E. H. (1946) *The Social Structure of the Southern Sotho Ward.* Communications from the School of African Studies, n.s. 15. University of Cape Town.

ASHTON, E. H. (1967) *The Basuto* (second edition). London: Oxford University Press for International African Institute.

ATMORE, A. (1969) 'The passing of Sotho independence', in Thompson (1969), 282–301.

BEARDSLEY, J. E. (1970) 'The common law in Lesotho', *Journal of African Law* 14, 3: 198–202.

BECKER, P. (1969) *Hill of Destiny.* London: Longmans.

BLACKSTONE, W. (1783) *Commentaries on the Laws of England* (ninth edition).

BOHANNAN, P. (1957) *Justice and Judgment among the Tiv.* London: Oxford University Press for International African Institute.

CASALIS, E. (1930) *Les Bassoutos.* Paris: Société des Missions Evangéliques (first published 1859).

DICEY, A. V. (1948) *Introduction to the Study of the Law of the Constitution* (ninth edition, with an introduction and appendix by E. C. S. Wade). London: Macmillan (first published 1885).

DOKE, C. M. (1954) *The Southern Bantu Languages.* London: Oxford University Press for International African Institute.

DOKE, C. M. and MOFOKENG, S. M. (1957) *Textbook of Southern Sotho Grammar.* London and Cape Town: Longmans, Green.

DOUGLAS, M. (1970) *Natural Symbols.* London: Barrie & Rockliff, The Cresset Press.

DUNCAN, P. D. (1960) *Sotho Laws and Customs.* Cape Town: Oxford University Press.

DURKHEIM, E. (1912) *Les Formes élémentaires de la vie religieuse.* Paris: F. Alcan.

EISENSTADT, S. N. (1959) 'Primitive political systems: a preliminary comparative analysis', *American Anthropologist* 61: 200–20.

156

ELLENBERGER, D. F. and MACGREGOR, J. C. (1912) *History of the Basuto, Ancient and Modern.* London: Caxton Publishing Company.

FALLERS, L. A. (1955) 'The predicament of the modern African chief: an instance from Uganda', *American Anthropologist* 57: 290–304.

FALLERS, L. A. (1965) *Bantu Bureaucracy.* University of Chicago Press.

FALLERS, L. A. (1969) *Law without Precedent.* University of Chicago Press.

FRANK, J. (1949) *Law and the Modern Mind.* London: Stevens (first published 1930).

FRIEDMANN, W. (1967) Legal Theory (fifth edition). London: Stevens.

GERMOND, R. C. (ed.) (1967) *Chronicles of Basutoland.* Morija, Lesotho: Morija Sesuto Book Depot.

GIDDENS, A. (1968) ' "Power" in the recent writings of Talcott Parsons', *Sociology* 2: 257–72.

GLUCKMAN, M. (1943) *Essays on Lozi Land and Royal Property.* Livingstone: Rhodes-Livingstone Institute. Paper No. 10.

GLUCKMAN, M. (1955) *The Judicial Process among the Barotse of Northern Rhodesia.* Manchester University Press for the Rhodes-Livingstone Institute.

GLUCKMAN, M. (1965) *The Ideas in Barotse Jurisprudence.* New Haven and London: Yale University Press.

GLUCKMAN, M. (1967) *The Judicial Process among the Barotse of Northern Rhodesia (Zambia)* (second enlarged edition of Gluckman (1955)). Manchester University Press.

GLUCKMAN, M. (1972) second edition of Gluckman (1965), with new preface. Manchester University Press for Institute of Social Research, Zambia.

GLUCKMAN, M. (1973) third edition of Gluckman (1955) and (1967), with new preface. Manchester University Press.

GLUCKMAN, M. (ed.) (1969) *Ideas and Procedures in African Customary Law.* London: Oxford University Press for International African Institute.

GOODY, J. (ed.) (1966) *Succession to High Office* (Cambridge Papers in Social Anthropology No. 4). Cambridge University Press for the Department of Archaeology and Anthropology.

GUEST, A. G. (ed.) (1961) *Oxford Essays in Jurisprudence.* London: Oxford University Press.

GULLIVER, P. H. (1963) *Social Control in an African Society.* London: Routledge & Kegan Paul.

GULLIVER, P. H. (1969a) 'Case studies of law in non-Western societies', in Nader (1969), 11–23.

GULLIVER, P. H. (1969b) 'Dispute settlement without courts: the Ndendeuli of Southern Tanzania', in Nader (1969), 24–68.

HAILEY, LORD (1953) *Native Administration in the British African Territories. Part V: The High Commission Territories.* London: HMSO.

HALPERN, J. (1965) *South Africa's Hostages.* Harmondsworth: Penguin Books.

HAMNETT, I. (1965) 'Koena chieftainship seniority in Basutoland', *Africa* 35: 241–51.

HAMNETT, I. (1967a) Review of Ashton (1967) and Stevens (1967), *Race*, 9: 260–1.

HAMNETT, I. (1967b) 'Ambiguity, classification and change: the function of riddles', *Man*, n.s. 2: 379–93.

HAMNETT, I. (1970) 'Sotho law and custom in Basutoland', Ph.D. thesis, University of Edinburgh.

HAMNETT, I. (1971) 'Some notes on the concept of custom in Lesotho', *Journal of African Law*, 15: 3.

HAMNETT, I. (1973a) 'Some problems in the assessment of land shortage: a case study in Lesotho', *African Affairs* 72, no. 286: 37–45.

HAMNETT, I. (1973b) 'Legal change in Lesotho', *Rural Africana* 22: 83–91.

HUGHES, A. J. B. (1964) *Swazi Land Tenure*. Institute of Social Research, University of Natal.

JONES, G. I. (1951) *Basutoland Medicine Murders*. Cmd 8209. London: HMSO.

JONES, G. I. (1966) 'Chiefly succession in Basutoland', in Goody (1966), 57–81.

KELSEN, H (1934) 'The pure theory of law—its methods and fundamental concepts', *Law Quarterly Review* 50 (1934): 474ff. and 51 (1935): 517ff.

KUPER, A. (1970) *Kalahari Village Politics* (Cambridge Studies in Social Anthropology No. 3). Cambridge University Press.

KUPER, A. (1971) 'Council structure and decision making', in Richards and Kuper (1971), 13–28.

KUPER, H. (1947) *An African Aristocracy*. London: Oxford University Press for International African Institute.

KUPER, H. and KUPER, L. (eds) (1965) *African Law: Adaptation and Development*. Berkeley and Los Angeles: University of California Press.

LAGDEN, G. (1909) *The Basutos* (two volumes). London: Hutchinson.

LEENHARDT, M. (1939) 'La notion de mariage au Basutoland', *Bulletin des Missions* (St-André-Lez-Bruges), 18, 1: 99–104.

LEGASSICK, M. (1969) 'The Sotho-Tswana peoples before 1800', in Thompson (1969), 86–125.

LEVI, E. H. (1948) *An Introduction to Legal Reasoning*. University of Chicago Press.

LOUCH, A. R. (1966) *Explanation and Human Action*. Oxford: Basil Blackwell.

LYE, W. (1969) 'The distribution of the Sotho peoples after the Difaqane', in Thompson (1969), 191–206.

MAINE, SIR H. (1950) *Ancient Law*. London: Oxford University Press (first published 1861).

MAIR, L. (1962) *Primitive Government*. Harmondsworth: Penguin Books.

MALINOWSKI, B. (1926) *Crime and Custom in Savage Society*. London: Routledge & Kegan Paul.

MARSHALL, G. (1961) 'Justiciability', in Guest (1961), 265–87.

MOORE, S. F. (1970) 'Politics, procedures and norms in changing Chagga law', *Africa* 40: 321–44.

MOROJELE, C. M. H. (1962, etc.) *1960 Agricultural Census Reports* (eight parts). Maseru, Lesotho: Department of Agriculture.

MOSHESH, N. (1880) *A Little Light from Basutoland.* Cape Town: privately printed (J. M. Orpen?).

NADER, L. (ed.) (1969) *Law in Culture and Society.* Chicago: Aldine Press.

PALMER, V. (1970) *The Roman-Dutch and Sesotho Law of Delict.* Leiden: A. W. Sijthoff.

PALMER, V. and POULTER, S. (1972) *The Legal System of Lesotho.* Charlottesville, Va.: Michie.

PAROZ, R. A. (1957) *Elements of Southern Sotho* (revised edition). Morija: Morija Sesuto Book Depot.

PAROZ, R. A. (1961) *Southern Sotho-English Dictionary* by A. Mabille and H. Dieterlen, reclassified, revised and enlarged by R. A. Paroz. Morija: Morija Sesuto Book Depot.

PARSONS, T. (1954) *Essays in Sociological Theory* (revised edition). Chicago: Free Press.

PARSONS, T. (1960) *Structure and Process in Industrial Societies.* Chicago: Free Press.

PLUCKNETT, T. F. T. (1949) *Legislation of Edward I.* Oxford: Clarendon Press.

POPPER, SIR K. R. (1962) *The Open Society and its Enemies* (fourth edition), volume I. London: Routledge & Kegan Paul.

POTHOLM, C. P. and DALE, R. (eds) (1972) *Southern Africa in Perspective.* New York: Free Press.

POULTER, S. (1969) 'The common law in Lesotho', *Journal of African Law* 13: 127–44.

POULTER, S. (1972) 'The place of the Laws of Lerotholi in the legal system of Lesotho', *African Affairs* 71, no. 283: 144ff.

POUND, R. (1923) 'The theory of judicial decision', *Harvard Law Review* 34, 35 and 36.

PROCTOR, J. H. (1969) 'Building a constitutional monarchy in Lesotho', *Civilisations* 19: 64ff.

RAMOLEFE, A. M. R. (n.d.) 'The Restatement of Sesotho Customary Law: the Law of Marriage'. University of London Restatement of African Law Project (not published).

RAMOLEFE, A. M. R. (1969) 'Sesotho marriage, guardianship and the customary-law heir', in Gluckman (1969), 196–209.

RAMOLEFE, A. M. R. (1970) 'Lesotho', in Allott (1970), 248–60, 311.

RICHARDS, A. and KUPER, A. (eds) (1971) *Councils in Action* (Cambridge Studies in Social Anthropology No. 6). Cambridge University Press.

SAHLINS, M. D. (1961) 'The segmentary lineage—an organization for predatory expansion', *American Anthropologist* 63: 322–45.

SALMOND, SIR J. (1947) *Jurisprudence* (tenth edition by Glanville R. Williams). London: Sweet & Maxwell.

SAWER, W. (1965) *Law in Society.* Oxford: Clarendon Press.

SCHAPERA, I. (1955) *A Handbook of Tswana Law and Custom* (second edition). London: Oxford University Press for International African Institute.

SHAPIRO, D. L. (1965) 'The choice of rule making or adjudication in the development of administrative policy', *Harvard Law Review* 78: 921ff.

SHEDDICK, V. G. J. (1953) *The Southern Sotho*. Ethnographic Survey of Africa, Southern Africa, Part Two. London: International African Institute.

SHEDDICK, V. G. J. (1954) *Land Tenure in Basutoland* (Colonial Research Studies No. 13). London: HMSO.

SMITH, M. G. (1956) 'On segmentary lineage systems', *J. R. Anthrop. Inst.* 86: 37–80.

SMITH, M. G. (1960) *Government in Zazzau 1800–1950*. London: Oxford University Press for International African Institute.

SMITH, M. G. (1965) 'The sociological framework of law', in Kuper and Kuper (1965), 24–48.

SPENCE, J. E. (1968) *Lesotho: the Politics of Dependence*. London: Oxford University Press for Institute of Race Relations.

STEVENS, R. P. (1967) *Lesotho, Botswana and Swaziland*. London: Pall Mall Press.

STONE, J. (1964) *Legal System and Lawyers' Reasonings*. London: Stevens.

STONE, J. (1966) *Law and the Social Sciences in the Second Half Century*. Minneapolis: University of Minnesota Press.

THOMPSON, L. (ed.) (1969) *African Societies in Southern Africa*. London: Heinemann.

TYLDEN, G. (1950) *The Rise of the Basuto*. Cape Town and Johannesburg: Juta.

VANDERLINDEN, J. (1966) 'A propos de quelques ouvrages récents de droit africain', *Africa* 36: 359–72.

VANDERLINDEN, J. (1969) 'Réflexions sur l'existence du concept de propriété immobilière individuelle dans les droits africains traditionels', in Gluckman (1969), 236–51.

WADE, E. C. S. (1961) *Administrative Law*. Oxford: Clarendon Press.

WALLMAN, S. (1965) 'The communication of measurement in Basutoland', *Human Organization* 24, 3.

WALLMAN, S. (1969) *Take Out Hunger* (LSE Monographs in Social Anthropology No. 39). London: Athlone Press.

WEBER, M. (1947) *The Theory of Social and Economic Organisation* (English translation by A. H. Henderson and T. Parsons) New York: Oxford University Press.

WEBER, M. (1954) *Law in Economy and Society*, edited by M. Rheinstein. Cambridge, Mass.: Harvard University Press.

WEISFELDER, R. F. (1969) *Defining National Purpose in Lesotho* (Papers in International Studies, Africa Series, No. 3). Athens, Ohio: Ohio University Center for International Studies.

WEISFELDER, R. F. (1972a) *The Basotho Monarchy* (Papers in International Studies, Africa Series, No. 16). Athens, Ohio: Ohio University Center for International Studies.

WEISFELDER, R. F. (1972b) 'Lesotho', in Potholm and Dale (1972), 125–40.

WILSON, M. and THOMPSON, L. (eds) (1969) *The Oxford History of South Africa, Volume One, South Africa to 1870*. Oxford: Clarendon Press.

WILSON, N. (1965) 'The sociology of a profession: the Faculty of Advocates', Ph.D. thesis, University of Edinburgh.

Index

Allocation: of cattle and goods, 51, 55f., 59f., 122, 140; of Land, *see* Land, allocation of
Allott, A. N., 11
Arbitration, courts of, 94f.
Ashton, E. H., 41, 69, 143, 144, 152
Atmore, A., 136, 144, 145, 146

Basotho Courts (Basuto Courts), 6, 48, 56, 60–2, 64f., 76f., 79f., 83f., 91f., 95, 106, 148, 154
Basutoland, *see* Lesotho
Batson, E., 145
Beardsley, J. E., 152
Becker, P., 145
Blackstone, W., 102
Bohali, 41, 48, 58, 111f., 122f., 129, 153f., 154f.; *see also* Cattle
Bohannan, P., 107
Bridewealth, *see Bohali*
Butler, Samuel, 105

Case records, 6f., 16
Cattle, 2f., 45f., 53f., 57, 64, 87f., 123, 130, 152; *see also Bohali*
Chiefs and chieftainship, 4f., 15, 21f., Ch. 2 *passim*, 45, 53, 63f., 71–84, Ch. 5 *passim*, 106f., 108f., 113f., 145, 146f., 150, 151
Chieftainship succession, 23, Ch. 2 *passim*, 45, 49, Appendix 1 *passim*, 137, 145
Commission on Native Laws and Customs (1873), 53f., 149
Conciliation as court function, 20, 144

Devlin, Lord, 105
Dicey, A. V., 152
Differentiation of function, 21f., 110–113

Discretion, 18, 61, 65, 77, 78f., 81, 94, 99, 113, 115, 131, 144
Douglas, M., 1
Duncan, P. D., 36, 38, 39, 143, 152
Durkheim, E., 114

Eisenstadt, S. N., 103
Erewhon and 'musical banks', 105

Fallers, L. A., 6f., 16, 18f., 90, 107–10, 144
Family councils, 13, 39f., 49–51, 56, 93f., 116, 130f., 140
Frank, J., 102
Friedmann, W., 153

Gardens and sites, 71f., 82ff., 138
Germond, R. C., 145
Giddens, A., 104
Gluckman, M., 15–19, 20, 30, 143, 144, 147, 148, 150, 151, 152, 153
Gulliver, P. H., 7, 19ff., 109, 143, 144

Hailey, Lord, 143, 144
Halpern, J., 88, 143
Hamnett, I., 10, 69, 143, 144, 145, 150
Houses (*malapa*), 38, 46, 58ff., 70, 127, 137, 139f., 146
Hughes, A. J. B., 65

Inheritance: private succession and, 13, 23, Ch. 3 *passim*, 85, 93f., 98, 115, 122, 127f., 139f., 147; widows and heirs, 23, 47, 48, 53ff., 80, 85, 140, 149

Jonathan, Chief Leabua, 5, 143
Jones, G. I., 36, 143, 144, 146, 154
Judicial and administrative courts and processes, 36, 52f., 76, 78, 81f., 90–101, Conclusion *passim*, 147, 148,

161

Routledge Social Science Series

Routledge & Kegan Paul   London and Boston
68–74 Carter Lane   London EC4V 5EL
9 Park Street   Boston   Mass 02108

Contents

Authors wishing to submit manuscripts for any series in
this catalogue should send them to the Social Science Editor,
Routledge & Kegan Paul Ltd, 68–74 Carter Lane,
London EC4V 5EL

● *Books so marked are available in paperback*
All books are in Metric Demy 8vo format (216 × 138mm approx.)

International Library of Sociology

General Editor John Rex

GENERAL SOCIOLOGY

Barnsley, J. H. The Social Reality of Ethics. *464 pp.*
Belshaw, Cyril. The Conditions of Social Performance. *An Exploratory Theory. 144 pp.*
Brown, Robert. Explanation in Social Science. *208 pp.*
● Rules and Laws in Sociology. *192 pp.*
Bruford, W. H. Chekhov and His Russia. *A Sociological Study. 244 pp.*
Cain, Maureen E. Society and the Policeman's Role. *326 pp.*
Gibson, Quentin. The Logic of Social Enquiry. *240 pp.*
Glucksmann, M. Structuralist Analysis in Contemporary Social Thought. *212 pp.*
Gurvitch, Georges. Sociology of Law. *Preface by Roscoe Pound. 264 pp.*
Hodge, H. A. Wilhelm Dilthey. *An Introduction. 184 pp.*
Homans, George C. Sentiments and Activities. *336 pp.*
Johnson, Harry M. Sociology: *a Systematic Introduction. Foreword by Robert K. Merton. 710 pp.*
Mannheim, Karl. Essays on Sociology and Social Psychology. *Edited by Paul Kecskemeti. With Editorial Note by Adolph Lowe. 344 pp.*
Systematic Sociology: *An Introduction to the Study of Society. Edited by J. S. Erös and Professor W. A. C. Stewart. 220 pp.*
Martindale, Don. The Nature and Types of Sociological Theory. *292 pp.*
●**Maus, Heinz.** A Short History of Sociology. *234 pp.*
Mey, Harald. Field-Theory. *A Study of its Application in the Social Sciences. 352 pp.*
Myrdal, Gunnar. Value in Social Theory: *A Collection of Essays on Methodology. Edited by Paul Streeten. 332 pp.*
Ogburn, William F., and **Nimkoff, Meyer F.** A Handbook of Sociology. *Preface by Karl Mannheim. 656 pp. 46 figures. 35 tables.*
Parsons, Talcott, and **Smelser, Neil J.** Economy and Society: *A Study in the Integration of Economic and Social Theory. 362 pp.*
●**Rex, John.** Key Problems of Sociological Theory. *220 pp.*
Discovering Sociology. *278 pp.*
Sociology and the Demystification of the Modern World. *282 pp.*
●**Rex, John** (Ed.) Approaches to Sociology. *Contributions by Peter Abell, Frank Bechhofer, Basil Bernstein, Ronald Fletcher, David Frisby, Miriam Glucksmann, Peter Lassman, Herminio Martins, John Rex, Roland Robertson, John Westergaard and Jock Young. 302 pp.*
Rigby, A. Alternative Realities. *352 pp.*
Roche, M. Phenomenology, Language and the Social Sciences. *374 pp.*
Sahay, A. Sociological Analysis. *220 pp.*
Urry, John. Reference Groups and the Theory of Revolution. *244 pp.*
Weinberg, E. Development of Sociology in the Soviet Union. *173 pp.*

FOREIGN CLASSICS OF SOCIOLOGY

● **Durkheim, Emile.** Suicide. *A Study in Sociology. Edited and with an Introduction by George Simpson. 404 pp.*
Professional Ethics and Civic Morals. *Translated by Cornelia Brookfield. 288 pp.*
● **Gerth, H. H.,** and **Mills, C. Wright.** From Max Weber: *Essays in Sociology. 502 pp.*
● **Tönnies, Ferdinand.** Community and Association. (*Gemeinschaft und Gesellschaft.*) *Translated and Supplemented by Charles P. Loomis. Foreword by Pitirim A. Sorokin. 334 pp.*

SOCIAL STRUCTURE

Andreski, Stanislav. Military Organization and Society. *Foreword by Professor A. R. Radcliffe-Brown. 226 pp. 1 folder.*
Coontz, Sydney H. Population Theories and the Economic Interpretation. *202 pp.*
Coser, Lewis. The Functions of Social Conflict. *204 pp.*
Dickie-Clark, H. F. Marginal Situation: *A Sociological Study of a Coloured Group. 240 pp. 11 tables.*
Glaser, Barney, and **Strauss, Anselm L.** Status Passage. *A Formal Theory. 208 pp.*
Glass, D. V. (Ed.) Social Mobility in Britain. *Contributions by J. Berent, T. Bottomore, R. C. Chambers, J. Floud, D. V. Glass, J. R. Hall, H. T. Himmelweit, R. K. Kelsall, F. M. Martin, C. A. Moser, R. Mukherjee, and W. Ziegel. 420 pp.*
Jones, Garth N. Planned Organizational Change: *An Exploratory Study Using an Empirical Approach. 268 pp.*
Kelsall, R. K. Higher Civil Servants in Britain: *From 1870 to the Present Day. 268 pp. 31 tables.*
König, René. The Community. *232 pp. Illustrated.*
● **Lawton, Denis.** Social Class, Language and Education. *192 pp.*
McLeish, John. The Theory of Social Change: *Four Views Considered. 128 pp.*
Marsh, David C. The Changing Social Structure of England and Wales, 1871-1961. *288 pp.*
Mouzelis, Nicos. Organization and Bureaucracy. *An Analysis of Modern Theories. 240 pp.*
Mulkay, M. J. Functionalism, Exchange and Theoretical Strategy. *272 pp.*
Ossowski, Stanislaw. Class Structure in the Social Consciousness. *210 pp.*
Podgórecki, Adam. Law and Society. *About 300 pp.*

SOCIOLOGY AND POLITICS

Acton, T. A. Gypsy Politics and Social Change. *316 pp.*
Hechter, Michael. Internal Colonialism. *The Celtic Fringe in British National Development, 1536-1966. About 350 pp.*
Hertz, Frederick. Nationality in History and Politics: *A Psychology and Sociology of National Sentiment and Nationalism. 432 pp.*

Kornhauser, William. The Politics of Mass Society. *272 pp. 20 tables.*

Laidler, Harry W. History of Socialism. *Social-Economic Movements: An Historical and Comparative Survey of Socialism, Communism, Co-operation, Utopianism; and other Systems of Reform and Reconstruction. 992 pp.*

Lasswell, H. D. Analysis of Political Behaviour. *324 pp.*

Mannheim, Karl. Freedom, Power and Democratic Planning. *Edited by Hans Gerth and Ernest K. Bramstedt. 424 pp.*

Mansur, Fatma. Process of Independence. *Foreword by A. H. Hanson. 208 pp.*

Martin, David A. Pacifism: *an Historical and Sociological Study. 262 pp.*

Myrdal, Gunnar. The Political Element in the Development of Economic Theory. *Translated from the German by Paul Streeten. 282 pp.*

Wootton, Graham. Workers, Unions and the State. *188 pp.*

FOREIGN AFFAIRS: THEIR SOCIAL, POLITICAL AND ECONOMIC FOUNDATIONS

Mayer, J. P. Political Thought in France from the Revolution to the Fifth Republic. *164 pp.*

CRIMINOLOGY

Ancel, Marc. Social Defence: *A Modern Approach to Criminal Problems. Foreword by Leon Radzinowicz. 240 pp.*

Cain, Maureen E. Society and the Policeman's Role. *326 pp.*

Cloward, Richard A., and **Ohlin, Lloyd E.** Delinquency and Opportunity: *A Theory of Delinquent Gangs. 248 pp.*

Downes, David M. The Delinquent Solution. *A Study in Subcultural Theory. 296 pp.*

Dunlop, A. B., and **McCabe, S.** Young Men in Detention Centres. *192 pp.*

Friedlander, Kate. The Psycho-Analytical Approach to Juvenile Delinquency: *Theory, Case Studies, Treatment. 320 pp.*

Glueck, Sheldon, and **Eleanor.** Family Environment and Delinquency. *With the statistical assistance of Rose W. Kneznek. 340 pp.*

Lopez-Rey, Manuel. Crime. *An Analytical Appraisal. 288 pp.*

Mannheim, Hermann. Comparative Criminology: *a Text Book. Two volumes. 442 pp. and 380 pp.*

Morris, Terence. The Criminal Area: *A Study in Social Ecology. Foreword by Hermann Mannheim. 232 pp. 25 tables. 4 maps.*

Rock, Paul. Making People Pay. *338 pp.*

● **Taylor, Ian, Walton, Paul,** and **Young, Jock.** The New Criminology. *For a Social Theory of Deviance. 325 pp.*

SOCIAL PSYCHOLOGY

Bagley, Christopher. The Social Psychology of the Epileptic Child. *320 pp.*

Barbu, Zevedei. Problems of Historical Psychology. *248 pp.*

Blackburn, Julian. Psychology and the Social Pattern. *184 pp.*

●**Brittan, Arthur.** Meanings and Situations. *224 pp.*

Carroll, J. Break-Out from the Crystal Palace. *200 pp.*

●**Fleming, C. M.** Adolescence: Its Social Psychology. *With an Introduction to recent findings from the fields of Anthropology, Physiology, Medicine, Psychometrics and Sociometry. 288 pp.*

● The Social Psychology of Education: *An Introduction and Guide to Its Study. 136 pp.*

Homans, George C. The Human Group. *Foreword by Bernard DeVoto. Introduction by Robert K. Merton. 526 pp.*

● Social Behaviour: *its Elementary Forms. 416 pp.*

●**Klein, Josephine.** The Study of Groups. *226 pp. 31 figures. 5 tables.*

Linton, Ralph. The Cultural Background of Personality. *132 pp.*

●**Mayo, Elton.** The Social Problems of an Industrial Civilization. *With an appendix on the Political Problem. 180 pp.*

Ottaway, A. K. C. Learning Through Group Experience. *176 pp.*

Ridder, J. C. de. The Personality of the Urban African in South Africa. *A Thematic Apperception Test Study. 196 pp. 12 plates.*

●**Rose, Arnold M.** (Ed.) Human Behaviour and Social Processes: *an Interactionist Approach. Contributions by Arnold M. Rose, Ralph H. Turner, Anselm Strauss, Everett C. Hughes, E. Franklin Frazier, Howard S. Becker, et al. 696 pp.*

Smelser, Neil J. Theory of Collective Behaviour. *448 pp.*

Stephenson, Geoffrey M. The Development of Conscience. *128 pp.*

Young, Kimball. Handbook of Social Psychology. *658 pp. 16 figures. 10 tables.*

SOCIOLOGY OF THE FAMILY

Banks, J. A. Prosperity and Parenthood: *A Study of Family Planning among The Victorian Middle Classes. 262 pp.*

Bell, Colin R. Middle Class Families: *Social and Geographical Mobility. 224 pp.*

Burton, Lindy. Vulnerable Children. *272 pp.*

Gavron, Hannah. The Captive Wife: *Conflicts of Household Mothers. 190 pp.*

George, Victor, and **Wilding, Paul.** Motherless Families. *220 pp.*

Klein, Josephine. Samples from English Cultures.
　　1. Three Preliminary Studies and Aspects of Adult Life in England. *447 pp.*
　　2. Child-Rearing Practices and Index. *247 pp.*

Klein, Viola. Britain's Married Women Workers. *180 pp.*
　　The Feminine Character. *History of an Ideology. 244 pp.*

McWhinnie, Alexina M. Adopted Children. *How They Grow Up. 304 pp.*

● **Myrdal, Alva,** and **Klein, Viola.** Women's Two Roles: *Home and Work. 238 pp. 27 tables.*

Parsons, Talcott, and **Bales, Robert F.** Family: Socialization and Inter-action Process. *In collaboration with James Olds, Morris Zelditch and Philip E. Slater. 456 pp. 50 figures and tables.*

SOCIAL SERVICES

Bastide, Roger. The Sociology of Mental Disorder. *Translated from the French by Jean McNeil. 260 pp.*

Carlebach, Julius. Caring For Children in Trouble. *266 pp.*

Forder, R. A. (Ed.) Penelope Hall's Social Services of England and Wales. *352 pp.*

George, Victor. Foster Care. *Theory and Practice. 234 pp.*
Social Security: *Beveridge and After. 258 pp.*

George, V., and **Wilding, P.** Motherless Families. *248 pp.*

●**Goetschius, George W.** Working with Community Groups. *256 pp.*

Goetschius, George W., and **Tash, Joan.** Working with Unattached Youth. *416 pp.*

Hall, M. P., and **Howes, I. V.** The Church in Social Work. *A Study of Moral Welfare Work undertaken by the Church of England. 320 pp.*

Heywood, Jean S. Children in Care: *the Development of the Service for the Deprived Child. 264 pp.*

Hoenig, J., and **Hamilton, Marian W.** The De-Segregation of the Mentally Ill. *284 pp.*

Jones, Kathleen. Mental Health and Social Policy, 1845-1959. *264 pp.*

King, Roy D., Raynes, Norma V., and **Tizard, Jack.** Patterns of Residential Care. *356 pp.*

Leigh, John. Young People and Leisure. *256 pp.*

Morris, Mary. Voluntary Work and the Welfare State. *300 pp.*

Morris, Pauline. Put Away: *A Sociological Study of Institutions for the Mentally Retarded. 364 pp.*

Nokes, P. L. The Professional Task in Welfare Practice. *152 pp.*

Timms, Noel. Psychiatric Social Work in Great Britain (1939-1962). *280 pp.*

● Social Casework: *Principles and Practice. 256 pp.*

Young, A. F. Social Services in British Industry. *272 pp.*

Young, A. F., and **Ashton, E. T.** British Social Work in the Nineteenth Century. *288 pp.*

SOCIOLOGY OF EDUCATION

Banks, Olive. Parity and Prestige in English Secondary Education: a Study in Educational Sociology. *272 pp.*

Bentwich, Joseph. Education in Israel. *224 pp. 8 pp. plates.*

●**Blyth, W. A. L.** English Primary Education. *A Sociological Description.*
1. Schools. *232 pp.*
2. Background. *168 pp.*

Collier, K. G. The Social Purposes of Education: *Personal and Social Values in Education. 268 pp.*

7

Dale, R. R., and **Griffith, S.** Down Stream: *Failure in the Grammar School.* *108 pp.*

Dore, R. P. Education in Tokugawa Japan. *356 pp. 9 pp. plates.*

Evans, K. M. Sociometry and Education. *158 pp.*

●**Ford, Julienne.** Social Class and the Comprehensive School. *192 pp.*

Foster, P. J. Education and Social Change in Ghana. *336 pp. 3 maps.*

Fraser, W. R. Education and Society in Modern France. *150 pp.*

Grace, Gerald R. Role Conflict and the Teacher. *About 200 pp.*

Hans, Nicholas. New Trends in Education in the Eighteenth Century. *278 pp. 19 tables.*

● Comparative Education: *A Study of Educational Factors and Traditions.* *360 pp.*

Hargreaves, David. Interpersonal Relations and Education. *432 pp.*

● Social Relations in a Secondary School. *240 pp.*

Holmes, Brian. Problems in Education. *A Comparative Approach. 336 pp.*

King, Ronald. Values and Involvement in a Grammar School. *164 pp.*

School Organization and Pupil Involvement. *A Study of Secondary Schools.*

●**Mannheim, Karl,** and **Stewart, W. A. C.** An Introduction to the Sociology of Education. *206 pp.*

Morris, Raymond N. The Sixth Form and College Entrance. *231 pp.*

●**Musgrove, F.** Youth and the Social Order. *176 pp.*

●**Ottaway, A. K. C.** Education and Society: An Introduction to the Sociology of Education. *With an Introduction by W. O. Lester Smith. 212 pp.*

Peers, Robert. Adult Education: *A Comparative Study. 398 pp.*

Pritchard, D. G. Education and the Handicapped: *1760 to 1960. 258 pp.*

Richardson, Helen. Adolescent Girls in Approved Schools. *308 pp.*

Stratta, Erica. The Education of Borstal Boys. *A Study of their Educational Experiences prior to, and during, Borstal Training. 256 pp.*

Taylor, P. H., Reid, W. A., and **Holley, B. J.** The English Sixth Form. *A Case Study in Curriculum Research. 200 pp.*

SOCIOLOGY OF CULTURE

Eppel, E. M., and **M.** Adolescents and Morality: *A Study of some Moral Values and Dilemmas of Working Adolescents in the Context of a changing Climate of Opinion. Foreword by W. J. H. Sprott. 268 pp. 39 tables.*

●**Fromm, Erich.** The Fear of Freedom. *286 pp.*

● The Sane Society. *400 pp.*

Mannheim, Karl. Essays on the Sociology of Culture. *Edited by Ernst Mannheim in co-operation with Paul Kecskemeti. Editorial Note by Adolph Lowe. 280 pp.*

Weber, Alfred. Farewell to European History: *or The Conquest of Nihilism. Translated from the German by R. F. C. Hull. 224 pp.*

SOCIOLOGY OF RELIGION

Argyle, Michael and **Beit-Hallahmi, Benjamin.** The Social Psychology of Religion. *About 256 pp.*

Nelson, G. K. Spiritualism and Society. *313 pp.*

Stark, Werner. The Sociology of Religion. *A Study of Christendom.*
Volume I. *Established Religion. 248 pp.*
Volume II. *Sectarian Religion. 368 pp.*
Volume III. *The Universal Church. 464 pp.*
Volume IV. *Types of Religious Man. 352 pp.*
Volume V. *Types of Religious Culture. 464 pp.*

Turner, B. S. Weber and Islam. *216 pp.*

Watt, W. Montgomery. Islam and the Integration of Society. *320 pp.*

SOCIOLOGY OF ART AND LITERATURE

Jarvie, Ian C. Towards a Sociology of the Cinema. *A Comparative Essay on the Structure and Functioning of a Major Entertainment Industry. 405 pp.*

Rust, Frances S. Dance in Society. *An Analysis of the Relationships between the Social Dance and Society in England from the Middle Ages to the Present Day. 256 pp. 8 pp. of plates.*

Schücking, L. L. The Sociology of Literary Taste. *112 pp.*

Wulff, Janet. Hermeneutic Philosophy and the Sociology of Art. *About 200 pp.*

SOCIOLOGY OF KNOWLEDGE

Diesing, P. Patterns of Discovery in the Social Sciences. *262 pp.*

● **Douglas, J. D.** (Ed.) Understanding Everyday Life. *370 pp.*

● **Hamilton, P.** Knowledge and Social Structure. *174 pp.*

Jarvie, I. C. Concepts and Society. *232 pp.*

Mannheim, Karl. Essays on the Sociology of Knowledge. *Edited by Paul Kecskemeti. Editorial Note by Adolph Lowe. 353 pp.*

Remmling, Gunter W. (Ed.) Towards the Sociology of Knowledge. *Origin and Development of a Sociological Thought Style. 463 pp.*

Stark, Werner. The Sociology of Knowledge: *An Essay in Aid of a Deeper Understanding of the History of Ideas. 384 pp.*

URBAN SOCIOLOGY

Ashworth, William. The Genesis of Modern British Town Planning: *A Study in Economic and Social History of the Nineteenth and Twentieth Centuries. 288 pp.*

Cullingworth, J. B. Housing Needs and Planning Policy: *A Restatement of the Problems of Housing Need and 'Overspill' in England and Wales. 232 pp. 44 tables. 8 maps.*

Dickinson, Robert E. City and Region: *A Geographical Interpretation* *608 pp. 125 figures.*
The West European City: *A Geographical Interpretation.* *600 pp. 129 maps. 29 plates.*
● The City Region in Western Europe. *320 pp. Maps.*
Humphreys, Alexander J. New Dubliners: *Urbanization and the Irish Family. Foreword by George C. Homans. 304 pp.*
Jackson, Brian. Working Class Community: *Some General Notions raised by a Series of Studies in Northern England. 192 pp.*
Jennings, Hilda. Societies in the Making: *a Study of Development and Redevelopment within a County Borough. Foreword by D. A. Clark. 286 pp.*
●**Mann, P. H.** An Approach to Urban Sociology. *240 pp.*
Morris, R. N., and **Mogey, J.** The Sociology of Housing. *Studies at Berinsfield. 232 pp. 4 pp. plates.*
Rosser, C., and **Harris, C.** The Family and Social Change. *A Study of Family and Kinship in a South Wales Town. 352 pp. 8 maps.*

RURAL SOCIOLOGY

Chambers, R. J. H. Settlement Schemes in Tropical Africa: *A Selective Study. 268 pp.*
Haswell, M. R. The Economics of Development in Village India. *120 pp.*
Littlejohn, James. Westrigg: *the Sociology of a Cheviot Parish. 172 pp. 5 figures.*
Mayer, Adrian C. Peasants in the Pacific. *A Study of Fiji Indian Rural Society. 248 pp. 20 plates.*
Williams, W. M. The Sociology of an English Village: *Gosforth. 272 pp. 12 figures. 13 tables.*

SOCIOLOGY OF INDUSTRY AND DISTRIBUTION

Anderson, Nels. Work and Leisure. *280 pp.*
●**Blau, Peter M.,** and **Scott, W. Richard.** Formal Organizations: *a Comparative approach. Introduction and Additional Bibliography by J. H. Smith. 326 pp.*
Eldridge, J. E. T. Industrial Disputes. *Essays in the Sociology of Industrial Relations. 288 pp.*
Hetzler, Stanley. Applied Measures for Promoting Technological Growth. *352 pp.*
Technological Growth and Social Change. *Achieving Modernization. 269 pp.*
Hollowell, Peter G. The Lorry Driver. *272 pp.*
Jefferys, Margot, *with the assistance of Winifred Moss.* Mobility in the Labour Market: *Employment Changes in Battersea and Dagenham. Preface by Barbara Wootton. 186 pp. 51 tables.*

Millerson, Geoffrey. The Qualifying Associations: *a Study in Professionalization. 320 pp.*

Smelser, Neil J. Social Change in the Industrial Revolution: *An Application of Theory to the Lancashire Cotton Industry, 1770-1840. 468 pp. 12 figures. 14 tables.*

Williams, Gertrude. Recruitment to Skilled Trades. *240 pp.*

Young, A. F. Industrial Injuries Insurance: *an Examination of British Policy. 192 pp.*

DOCUMENTARY

Schlesinger, Rudolf (Ed.) Changing Attitudes in Soviet Russia.
2. The Nationalities Problem and Soviet Administration. *Selected Readings on the Development of Soviet Nationalities Policies. Introduced by the editor. Translated by W. W. Gottlieb. 324 pp.*

ANTHROPOLOGY

Ammar, Hamed. Growing up in an Egyptian Village: *Silwa, Province of Aswan. 336 pp.*

Brandel-Syrier, Mia. Reeftown Elite. *A Study of Social Mobility in a Modern African Community on the Reef. 376 pp.*

Crook, David, and Isabel. Revolution in a Chinese Village: *Ten Mile Inn. 230 pp. 8 plates. 1 map.*

Dickie-Clark, H. F. The Marginal Situation. *A Sociological Study of a Coloured Group. 236 pp.*

Dube, S. C. Indian Village. *Foreword by Morris Edward Opler. 276 pp. 4 plates.*
India's Changing Villages: *Human Factors in Community Development. 260 pp. 8 plates. 1 map.*

Firth, Raymond. Malay Fishermen. *Their Peasant Economy. 420 pp. 17 pp. plates.*

Firth, R., Hubert, J., and **Forge, A.** Families and their Relatives. *Kinship in a Middle-Class Sector of London: An Anthropological Study. 456 pp.*

Gulliver, P. H. Social Control in an African Society: a Study of the Arusha, Agricultural Masai of Northern Tanganyika. *320 pp. 8 plates. 10 figures.*
Family Herds. *288 pp.*

Ishwaran, K. Shivapur. *A South Indian Village. 216 pp.*
Tradition and Economy in Village India: *An Interactionist Approach. Foreword by Conrad Arensburg. 176 pp.*

Jarvie, Ian C. The Revolution in Anthropology. *268 pp.*

Jarvie, Ian C., and **Agassi, Joseph.** Hong Kong. *A Society in Transition. 396 pp. Illustrated with plates and maps.*

Little, Kenneth L. Mende of Sierra Leone. *308 pp. and folder.*
Negroes in Britain. *With a New Introduction and Contemporary Study by Leonard Bloom. 320 pp.*

Lowie, Robert H. Social Organization. *494 pp.*
Mayer, Adrian C. Caste and Kinship in Central India: *A Village and its Region. 328 pp. 16 plates. 15 figures. 16 tables.*
 Peasants in the Pacific. *A Study of Fiji Indian Rural Society. 248 pp.*
Smith, Raymond T. The Negro Family in British Guiana: *Family Structure and Social Status in the Villages. With a Foreword by Meyer Fortes. 314 pp. 8 plates. 1 figure. 4 maps.*

SOCIOLOGY AND PHILOSOPHY

Barnsley, John H. The Social Reality of Ethics. *A Comparative Analysis of Moral Codes. 448 pp.*
Diesing, Paul. Patterns of Discovery in the Social Sciences. *362 pp.*
●**Douglas, Jack D.** (Ed.) Understanding Everyday Life. *Toward the Reconstruction of Sociological Knowledge. Contributions by Alan F. Blum. Aaron W. Cicourel, Norman K. Denzin, Jack D. Douglas, John Heeren, Peter McHugh, Peter K. Manning, Melvin Power, Matthew Speier, Roy Turner, D. Lawrence Wieder, Thomas P. Wilson and Don H. Zimmerman. 370 pp.*
Jarvie, Ian C. Concepts and Society. *216 pp.*
Pelz, Werner. The Scope of Understanding in Sociology. *Towards a more radical reorientation in the social humanistic sciences. 283 pp.*
Roche, Maurice. Phenomenology, Language and the Social Sciences. *371 pp.*
Sahay, Arun. Sociological Analysis. *212 pp.*
Sklair, Leslie. The Sociology of Progress. *320 pp.*

International Library of Anthropology

General Editor Adam Kuper

Brown, Paula. The Chimbu. *A Study of Change in the New Guinea Highlands. 151 pp.*
Lloyd, P. C. Power and Independence. *Urban Africans' Perception of Social Inequality. 264 pp.*
Pettigrew, Joyce. Robber Noblemen. *A Study of the Political System of the Sikh Jats. 284 pp.*
Van Den Berghe, Pierre L. Power and Privilege at an African University. *278 pp.*

International Library of Social Policy

General Editor Kathleen Jones

Bayley, M. Mental Handicap and Community Care. *426 pp.*
Butler, J. R. Family Doctors and Public Policy. *208 pp.*
Holman, Robert. Trading in Children. *A Study of Private Fostering. 355 pp.*

Jones, Kathleen. History of the Mental Health Service. *428 pp.*
Thomas, J. E. The English Prison Officer since 1850: *A Study in Conflict.* *258 pp.*
Woodward, J. To Do the Sick No Harm. *A Study of the British Voluntary Hospital System to 1875. About 220 pp.*

International Library of Welfare and Philosophy

General Editors Noel Timms and David Watson

● **Plant, Raymond.** Community and Ideology. *104 pp.*

Primary Socialization, Language and Education

General Editor Basil Bernstein

Bernstein, Basil. Class, Codes and Control. *2 volumes.*
  1. *Theoretical Studies Towards a Sociology of Language. 254 pp.*
  2. *Applied Studies Towards a Sociology of Language. About 400 pp.*
Brandis, W., and **Bernstein, B.** Selection and Control. *176 pp.*
Brandis, Walter, and **Henderson, Dorothy.** Social Class, Language and Communication. *288 pp.*
Cook-Gumperz, Jenny. Social Control and Socialization. *A Study of Class Differences in the Language of Maternal Control. 290 pp.*
● **Gahagan, D. M.,** and **G. A.** Talk Reform. *Exploration in Language for Infant School Children. 160 pp.*
Robinson, W. P., and **Rackstraw, Susan D. A.** A Question of Answers. *2 volumes. 192 pp. and 180 pp.*
Turner, Geoffrey J., and **Mohan, Bernard A.** A Linguistic Description and Computer Programme for Children's Speech. *208 pp.*

Reports of the Institute of Community Studies

Cartwright, Ann. Human Relations and Hospital Care. *272 pp.*
● Parents and Family Planning Services. *306 pp.*
  Patients and their Doctors. *A Study of General Practice. 304 pp.*
● **Jackson, Brian.** Streaming: *an Education System in Miniature. 168 pp.*
Jackson, Brian, and **Marsden, Dennis.** Education and the Working Class: *Some General Themes raised by a Study of 88 Working-class Children in a Northern Industrial City. 268 pp. 2 folders.*
Marris, Peter. The Experience of Higher Education. *232 pp. 27 tables.*
  Loss and Change. *192 pp.*

Marris, Peter, and Rein, Martin. Dilemmas of Social Reform. *Poverty and Community Action in the United States. 256 pp.*

Marris, Peter, and Somerset, Anthony. African Businessmen. *A Study of Entrepreneurship and Development in Kenya. 256 pp.*

Mills, Richard. Young Outsiders: *a Study in Alternative Communities. 216 pp.*

Runciman, W. G. Relative Deprivation and Social Justice. *A Study of Attitudes to Social Inequality in Twentieth-Century England. 352 pp.*

Willmott, Peter. Adolescent Boys in East London. *230 pp.*

Willmott, Peter, and Young, Michael. Family and Class in a London Suburb. *202 pp. 47 tables.*

Young, Michael. Innovation and Research in Education. *192 pp.*

● Young, Michael, and McGeeney, Patrick. Learning Begins at Home. *A Study of a Junior School and its Parents. 128 pp.*

Young, Michael, and Willmott, Peter. Family and Kinship in East London. *Foreword by Richard M. Titmuss. 252 pp. 39 tables.*
The Symmetrical Family. *410 pp.*

Reports of the Institute for Social Studies in Medical Care

Cartwright, Ann, Hockey, Lisbeth, and Anderson, John L. Life Before Death. *310 pp.*

Dunnell, Karen, and Cartwright, Ann. Medicine Takers, Prescribers and Hoarders. *190 pp.*

Medicine, Illness and Society

General Editor W. M. Williams

Robinson, David. The Process of Becoming Ill. *142 pp.*

Stacey, Margaret, *et al.* Hospitals, Children and Their Families. *The Report of a Pilot Study. 202 pp.*

Monographs in Social Theory

General Editor Arthur Brittan

● Barnes, B. Scientific Knowledge and Sociological Theory. *About 200 pp.*

Bauman, Zygmunt. Culture as Praxis. *204 pp.*

● Dixon, Keith. Sociological Theory. *Pretence and Possibility. 142 pp.*

● Smith, Anthony D. The Concept of Social Change. *A Critique of the Functionalist Theory of Social Change. 208 pp.*

Routledge Social Science Journals

The British Journal of Sociology. *Edited by Terence P. Morris. Vol. 1, No. 1, March 1950 and Quarterly. Roy. 8vo. Back numbers available. An international journal with articles on all aspects of sociology.*
Economy and Society. *Vol. 1, No. 1. February 1972 and Quarterly. Metric Roy. 8vo. A journal for all social scientists covering sociology, philosophy, anthropology, economics and history. Back numbers available.*
Year Book of Social Policy in Britain, The. *Edited by Kathleen Jones. 1971. Published annually.*

Printed in Great Britain by Unwin Brothers Limited
The Gresham Press Old Woking Surrey
A member of the Staples Printing Group